DEDICATION

I dedicate this book to my lovely wife Florence and our children, Joyanna, David, Michelle, Robert, Dominic, and Terrence, whose understanding, sacrifices, and prayers made it possible for me to do my work. And I dedicate this book to the memory of my beloved mother, Cora Jones, who died at the age of ninety-nine years. She was always there to answer the many questions regarding my childhood during the writing of this book. Also, last but not least, to all people, everywhere, who are suffering from a life-threatening addiction.

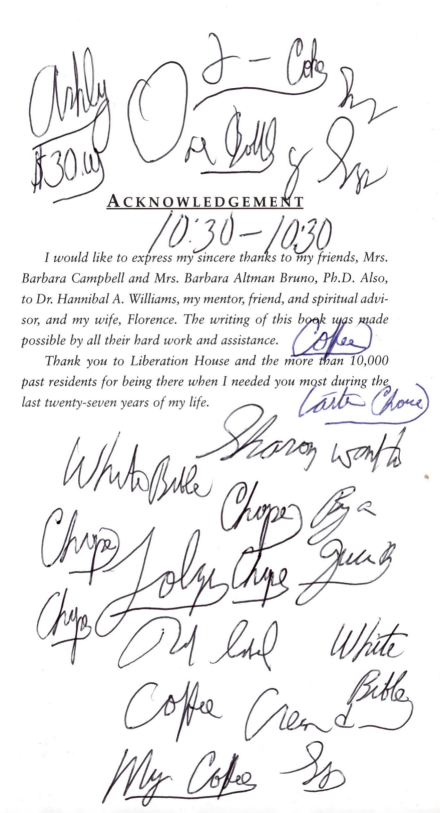

ACKNOWLEDGEMENT

I would like to express my sincere thanks to my friends, Mrs. Barbara Campbell and Mrs. Barbara Altman Bruno, Ph.D. Also, to Dr. Hannibal A. Williams, my mentor, friend, and spiritual advisor, and my wife, Florence. The writing of this book was made possible by all their hard work and assistance.

Thank you to Liberation House and the more than 10,000 past residents for being there when I needed you most during the last twenty-seven years of my life.

Sheep Sheep

8 Colp Book

Cough drops

Cough drops

Mints Mints

A Harmonica

A flute $5.00

Andrews

8 Color Book

PREFACE

Dr. Hannibal A. Williams

Liberation House is in part a product of the Liberation movement and revolution of the 1960s. It is also peculiarly related to the New Liberation Presbyterian Church. Both the church and the recovery home are the physical-material derivatives of a spiritual journey embarked on by a grateful alcoholic who woke up at midlife, with his life at an end.

Many blacks have been conditioned by the pervasive, constant racism dealt to the vast majority of black children born in this country. Racism had affected our social and economic standing, our physical and emotional health. In many ways we have been set up to be prone to alcoholism.

Nature has a hand: Just as blacks are more susceptible to sickle-cell anemia, and Jews to Tay-Sachs disease, blacks and Native Americans are more prone to alcoholism. Add to that the immeasurable psychological effect of the unrelenting racism which tells the American black that he is inferior to the other races, and you have the overwhelming conditioning to seek relief from the intolerable pain of degradation, humiliation, and futility. Alcohol affords relief and release, but such a relief is nullified by the slavery of addiction, with its corollary costs like degradation, loss of self-esteem, loss of health, job, memory, and more.

Somehow, in the foggy haze of my addiction, I got a glimmer of the light of truth, a realization of where I had come, and the eternal hope which is a part of all living organisms, and began to take the first faltering steps toward sanity. To whom or what institution could I turn? What establishment would help me, a black man?

The first obstacle I encountered was my blackness vis-à-vis society's institutions, which were totally geared to serving the white middle class. The more subtle, suggestive racism of cultural differences whispered to me, "Get out of here! This is not for you! Your vernacular is not spoken here!" While seeking the help of existing recovery facilities, I discovered sadly that racial prejudice was virulently active, not only in respectable white society, but even among whites who themselves were looked down on as reprehensible and incorrigible. There was still this critical distinction which proclaimed, "Not welcome!"

I experienced this rejection at a time when I had no defenses to protect the raw, exposed psyche of a sick, tired, tremulous being whose whole body, soul, and spirit craved the relief of one drink. I had been rebuffed at several existing facilities, even though they were recipients of public funding. Their excuse was, "Capacity occupied." Yet in a test case, a white man who followed me applied and was accepted.

As my friend Curtis Jones avers, all white folks are not mean; some are well-meaning. I sought the help of the central office of Alcoholics Anonymous, and a gruff, old, silver-haired white gentlelady named Harriet sat me down in her office and listened to my tale of woe. Following my sharing, she told me of a place located in the Hell's Kitchen of San Francisco's black ghetto, in the Fillmore District.

I didn't care! I wanted a place to lay a weary head, a haven of sobriety. I had tasted the hell of alcohol addiction, done time in county jail, and desperately wanted not to return to that lake of fire. The place where Harriet sent me was a real slum. It was not a house, just a large apartment. There were four bunk beds in a room, with little room for anything else. It was a flophouse, and I flopped down in it. Wonder of wonders, there was the camaraderie of fellow alcoholics, and they did not drink!

The rule of this haven-of-last-resort was six weeks' stay. You had to get a job within two days. You paid for your board. You stayed clean and sober. You attended AA meetings daily, and you didn't talk back or get smart. The place was a dump. If you stayed, you got dumped on. I stayed, and my sobriety was born!

To make a long story short, in my sobriety I was able to achieve the college education which had always eluded me. I was accepted to a Presbyterian seminary, where I received a Master's of Divinity and a Doctorate in Ministry. The denomination employed me to be the organizing pastor of a new church ministry in the black community of the Fillmore District of San Francisco. I found myself back on the same turf that I had roamed as a drunk and a ne'er-do-well.

Out of this venture, New Liberation Church was born. Out of the perceived need of a black alcoholic for a respectable recovery facility geared to his own cultural roots and social climate, Liberation House emerged.

As a pastor and a very busy social advocate, I could only give limited time to the project. I met this man, Curtis Jones, who was suffering a rebirth similar to my own. Mr. Jones made this project his own instrument of recovery. He rapidly became my partner in the organizing and development of Liberation House. At first he was dependent upon me for direction and motivation, but his growth was rapid, and soon I was depending on him for every aspect of the development of Liberation House. He progressively assumed more and more of the responsibility and grew apace. The project became his "baby." He made it; it made him!

Thus was Liberation House born, and thus was born to it a guy named Curtis Jones, who came in himself—like me—trembling, shaking, and very insecure, who caught the ball and ran with it. Well, that's his story, and that's history. I recommend it to all who may learn and profit thereby. Liberation House is literally a monument to the perseverance and determination of Mr. Curtis Jones, and I salute him.

I was born is a little country town north of Houston named Goodrich, Texas, on May 15, 1931. I was the fifth of seven children, five girls and two boys. My mother could read and was very smart. My father worked a big farm for its owner, a white man. He was the only hand who lived on the property; the other hands were hired from other parts of the county. Other white farm owners hired people to pick cotton and paid them a small fee. They called it "working on half"—whatever the hired people made, they split fifty-fifty with the farm owner. At the end of the crop year the farm owner was to split in half whatever money was netted with the Negroes who had worked the land. The Negroes had to furnish the seed for planting, labor, and tools. The bad part of working on half was that people who worked on half never caught up. They would always have to buy their supplies in the stores owned by the farm owners. The owners would tally up the cost of the supplies, and at the end of the crop season you always owed money to the owner.

My dad, having one of the better jobs, also helped drive his boss's Model T car. He was good at building and fixing things, as were his ancestors. His great-grandfather, a full-blooded Indian with long, plaited hair, was a master wagon builder. He moved from place to place—Meridian, Oklahoma; Texas, wherever. I think his son, my father's father, lived in Texas; he had passed away before my time. Dad could calculate numbers, but since he couldn't read or write, he wasn't able to make much money. Having been the oldest child of a large family, Dad had to go to work to support his mother and siblings after his own father died.

3

Where my father lived was called the prairie, and where my mother's father lived was called the bottom, by Trinity River and Long Cane Creek. There's rich land down there. My father bequeathed the land to us and we family members are still paying taxes on the land, which has remained vacant and is now overgrown with trees and bushes. No one wants to sell it because my uncle told us there was oil still in the ground.

My mother side of the family had a mixed bloodline. I'm not certain what the mixture was; I think it had something to do with English or Spanish. They were always able to trace their line. My mother's mother died, and her father remarried; that lady was always considered my grandmother. Grandfather had huge amounts of land owned by our family. My mother's half-brother is still staying there, though his wife died in 1992. Some oil company found oil and capped it up, and then said there was nothing there. But my uncle was well-schooled on that type of thing, and he found out about the oil. If a white person's land was nearby, the oil company would dig on the white person's land, cap it up on our land, and put an oil well over there so that we would not get any royalties. There was always a catch.

I remember helping open the gate for Dad and the boss to take the cows to the dipping vat, where the cows would swim to be rid of fleas and ticks. We children helped work the farm, even when it was very hot outside, and we were always late for school, starting in October after the crops finished. Cotton, corn, sugarcane, and peanuts were the crops, along with a small dairy herd, chickens, hogs, and a vegetable garden. When it came time to kill a hog, we would feed it all the leftover slop in order to fatten it, then Dad would shoot it, pour hot water on it, and scrape off the hair. My chores included feeding the chickens, helping Dad feed the horses, and pumping water. One of the chores that was traumatic to me was having to drown the litters of puppies and kittens.

As a kid, before my Daddy's boss died, we were the only ones in the immediate neighborhood who had a radio. Saturday nights in the country were great fun because all the neighbors came over and we'd gather around the radio to listen to the Grand Ol' Opry. I can remember a person who always came on, Cousin Minnie Pearl. She was the star of the show. She would be yelling and joking the whole time along with the Smokey Mountain Boys, the Carter Family, Ernie Ford, and so many others who were stars during the early 1940s. We just sat around the radio. We hadn't much to share but we baked potatoes in the ashes from the chimney. We'd take sweet potatoes and stick them into the ashes, and gee, those things were good! I can still taste that juice running through. All that stuff went away when he died. I don't even know what happened to the radio, but I remember listening to Joe Louis fights.

When the farm owner became ill and passed away, he left Dad six acres of land, two houses, a beautiful horse, two or three cows (including a good milk cow), and a set of mules. I was about six or seven at the time. The owner's daughter was married to a greedy man named Weeks. Weeks decided he wanted the best milk cow and the horse, and took them from my Dad. There wasn't much Dad could do about it then, because black people were not considered equal to white people. I watched my Dad die mentally. I could see the hurt in his eyes. I could see the whipping that he took, not being able to be a man and stand up and fight this man.

Tonya, We got Dad 10:30 AM Halloween god Cong God Bless you

I think the last shot that we had with Weeks involved a bowl that my mother had that she used at Christmastime to put fruit in. It was one of those collector's item types, and Weeks wanted it. He put up his wife to ask my mother for it, or to force my mother. My mother was good-hearted, and looked at it as being a good Samaritan doing a good thing, and was going to give it to her. That's when we kids intervened. "No, no. We won't do it!" So she didn't; she said, "No, we're not gonna give it to you. I've changed my mind."

Another traumatic memory involved the white families who lived next to the land my father's boss left my father. The land was where Shell Oil had oil storage tanks. One of the two families who lived right there had two boys a little bit older than I, who had all the good things like tricycles and bicycles, and I could never have any of those things. One of the brothers was named Richard and one was named Herman. Herman was more liberal and would let me ride behind him on his bicycle. We'd ride out on this country road and Richard would get a little tired of me hanging around and he'd say, "Well, let's sic the dog on him." They'd tell me to run on home and then they'd sic the dog, and then I'd have to climb up a tree because the dog scared me to death. I guess that's why I'm still afraid of dogs.

Right around the time I was going to the field with my sisters, too small to do anything, something else traumatic happened which my mother explained. At that time, they used Piper Cub planes to fly over pipelines to check them for damage or to see if they needed repairs. One of those planes flew so close to where I was standing that I could see the pilot and feel the sweep of the wind. The pipeline wasn't anywhere near. What he was really doing was looking for this man named Bob White who was working for another white person near Livingston. Bob White was a black man who was his boss's right-hand man.

The boss was supposed to go on a trip but for some reason canceled his trip and returned home. Bob White was never supposed to go into the boss's house, but for some reason had been invited in by the boss's wife. He was in the house when unexpectedly the boss returned home. The wife was surprised to see her husband, and Bob White, fearing for his life, ran out of the house. The boss asked his wife what Bob was doing in the house and she said he was trying to rape her.

So then they put out this big search for him. The sheriff said he was going to bring him in alive if it was the last thing he did. So the sheriff's men were circling over us to see if Bob was where we were.

[handwritten inscription: "To Bob $20.00" and signatures "Julia Game Game", "Chris Jeff"]

F inally, Bob surrendered, and the sheriff put him in jail in the middle of Livingston, Texas. The blacks got reports by word of mouth of what was going on there. You'd hear that they'd pulled Bob's fingernails out. That they were burning him with cigarettes. And then the big shocker was that they castrated him.

Finally they had his trial. A bird appeared, whistling the name "Bob White." The prosecution could not pin anything on Bob. The boss was so furious that he said, "No nigger'll ever get away with anything like this," and shot Bob White right in the courtroom. Nothing ever came of that—they just said he went crazy, lost his head, and shot Bob White.

As a result of this event so many questions began to form in my mind. Am I human or am I not? What kind of system is this? Am I in the wrong place? Will this happen to my dad, my brother, or will it happen to me? My mother said that God will take care of His people, but there is totally no justice in the way Negroes are being treated. There must be some better way than this. It was like a war zone, and the war zone was not only there. It moved wherever I moved.

Actually, when you stayed on the other side of the tracks, our part of town, then you were only exposed to people within the race. Maybe they'd be teasing you or riding you about this and that. But once you crossed over the tracks to the other side, then that's when it was there, that line. You had the feeling you had to play the game. You really had to know when to say yes and when to shut up and when not to say anything, or when to laugh when it wasn't funny. I learned to live with that, but it was a very tense life. By the time you got back on the other side of the tracks where you belonged, you were a nervous wreck. Everything you were doing was real. I didn't like pretending in order to satisfy whatever tastes somebody else had. That had a very devastating effect on me; a lot of questions came into my mind.

[handwritten inscription]

There was this boss in Goodrich who had a worker called Jim. The boss was obviously going with Jim's wife. They conceived a girl, Rose. She was beautiful; she stood out in the classroom. There were other mixed kids there, but she especially stood out because she had blue eyes and straight, strawberry-blonde hair. You couldn't tell her from somebody white unless you knew who she was. I didn't really understand that until later, when my mother explained to me what happened. I said, "Where was the husband?" She said, "Well, we couldn't do anything about it because we weren't allowed to speak up." The only thing he could say was, "Yes, sir; no, sir." So whatever the boss decided he wanted to do, he did. And the wife went along with the party because she wanted everything to be smooth. She didn't want to wrinkle anything and get her husband killed. The only thing you could do was get yourself killed if you objected to it.

We only had one time a year to buy shoes and school clothes and things like that. We'd go to town. We had to catch the Greyhound bus and sit on the back seat, the long one that crossed the back. They had this card that they used to put on the buses, saying "For Whites Only" on it. Behind the "Whites Only" sign it said "Colored." So the driver would always have the sign all the way back to the long seat in the back, over the motor, and that's where you would sit, and if there weren't any seats there you had to stand up. You stood as close to the back seat as you possibly could. The bathrooms on the trip were segregated. The whites were inside and the colored would use outhouses in the field. There was no running water; it was just a smelly, fly-ridden, open dump.

The water fountains were for whites only. If you went around to the side, there might be a hose or something connected to get a drink of water. If there actually was a water fountain for blacks and you could find it at all, it was isolated. If you got hungry, you had to go to the back of the restaurant and knock on the back door where the kitchen was. Then the cook or someone would come and ask you what you wanted. The first thing I saw when I left Goodrich and went to Houston was when the bus would have a little stopover and people would get out, and I'd see some of the Negroes go to the back. By the time you eventually got your food, the bus was ready to go because the whites would go in first and get theirs right away, while you waited. By the time you got your food, the bus driver was saying, "Come on, let's go," and you had to try to eat it as best you could on the bus. Sometimes you just didn't eat.

We could never try on clothes and shoes; Mom had to guess what our sizes were. And most times the shoes would be too narrow. We always had to cut them on the side by the toe because we couldn't take them back. You felt so embarrassed; you hated to walk down the streets all dressed up with slit shoes. I guess our feet were so wide because we never wore shoes except the months that we went to school or on Sundays for church. My bare feet really did take a beating from the hot sand and the thorns and thistles.

My dad seldom whipped me. He would scream and curse or scold me, and even now I don't like folks screaming at me. My father would never pick up a switch or a strap. My mother did the whipping when I deserved it. There were uncles living close by. If I would do something wrong and my aunt saw me, she would paddle me and then send word to my mother, so she too would know whatever happened. Then my mother would give me another whipping. Or the teacher would send a note home with me after she had paddled me, and then my mother would make me go outside and get a switch so she could whip me. And I had better bring back a good one, because if you didn't bring back a good one, then the whipping was going to be twice as bad. I always got two whippings! Then, all a person had to say was, "Well, you know your son Curtis was out here doing that. I paddled him." And when I got home Mom said, "What did you do that for?" and I got another whipping. So that was the structure you had. You really felt connected to the community and you knew you were watched over by people. Now, I wish blacks as a whole could experience that type of thing today. It would be better for them. You live next door to people now and they don't care what you do. Or if you go tell a mother, she might jump on you about reporting about her child.

We always supported one another. We were hungry because at times we had to eat biscuits and sugar water. That was a big drop. But people shared food. If we were out of something, we could borrow. Sometimes we never got it back. You didn't usually give back sugar, but maybe something else. Maybe you had potatoes. Whatever you had, you'd give it and say, "Well, I don't know when I'm gonna get this back. Here's some . . . " You just gave it.

I can remember the lady living across the street whom we called Cousin Ella. Her mother's name was Margaret, and she was very old—around a hundred. When she was a girl she had come from Africa with her people as slaves. She survived it. She would walk on a stick and tell us stories. Ella lived to be a hundred and two! She would always bring us gifts. They had this patch across from our house and she would raise potatoes, peanuts, watermelons, and she would always give big sacks of food to my mother and say, "Feed these kids." She talked to my sisters more than to me.

Cloudy Brown Sky / Been Side

My cousins and I—there was a group of nine or ten of us—would visit a man named Uncle Ike. Something had happened to him; he was almost blind. He would sit in this chair on his porch and we would go to hear him talk about the Bible and the stories about God, the devil, and things like that. A lot of things that you learn—wisdom from these old people you're around—never cost us anything but the time. They'd say, "You boys come and see me now," anytime we wanted. It was the openness there that I think kept a lot of hope alive, whereas when you went across the tracks you were back into some dreadful place. But this was an outlet here, people you circulated and visited with.

When you broke a bond, then you were expelled; you'd get out. I can remember when I was a young kid an incident that occurred with my Uncle Charles and the school principal, Mr. Higgins. People said that Mr. Higgins had got one of the girls pregnant. Although the girl was not related to my uncle, it affected him deeply because he had daughters who were the same age. He was so incited by this violation of trust that he took it upon himself to go to the leaders and men of the black community of Goodrich and insisted that this man had to go. Because of my uncle's stand, Mr. Higgins could no longer live in our community. He would have to marry the girl and leave. So the pressure was mounted against Mr. Higgins and he was fired. He left the area and went to California and sent for the girl. He took a job driving buses and lived a long time in California before he died. You see, it was forbidden to get a girl pregnant without being married to her. You were ostracized from the community. Due to my uncle's stand, other people began to take a stand. "We all have girls, and we can't have this. It could have been my girl."

My uncle wasn't necessarily a leader, but he would speak with boldness. He had nerve and guts. My mother told me that once some people had decided to whip him. He had sassed a doctor who owned the farm where my uncle worked. The doctor didn't like the smart answer that my uncle had given him, so he gathered a group of white people to go to his house with the intent of harming him. The doctor chose his best black workers to go with them to pull my uncle out of his house. They tried to frighten him to make him come out, but the two black men pretended that they saw a bear and ran off and left the whites alone. My uncle resisted and stood them off with his gun. So the whites built this big bonfire right in front of his house but they didn't do anything to him. The white men finally left and my uncle fled to our house. My dad hid him in our car and drove him out of town. My uncle had to stay away from that town for some years before he was able to return. Everybody within the neighborhood knew about what had happened. They were so afraid for my uncle. Incidents like these routinely resulted in the killing of a black.

15

O n my mother's side were the churchgoers. There were brothers—Uncle Perry, Uncle George—and they didn't let one outdo the other. Each one always sent one daughter to college. They worked hard. The only college close by was called Prairieview, near Houston. That's where most of them finished. Education was very important. My mom only finished about fifth grade. Her half-sister was a high-school teacher. Even the family members who didn't go to college could read. My father was the one who just never was able to read or write, but he was really mechanical, which seemed to make up in that era.

I remember this one cousin of mine, a teacher named Pearl. She lectured to us about smoking. I asked a few questions and said, "How do you know this thing's gonna harm me?" She said, "Well, I'm gonna bring a cigarette to school, and I'm gonna show you how this works." So the next day she brought a clean white handkerchief and a cigarette, which she lit. She puffed on the cigarette and blew smoke into the handkerchief and showed me the nicotine that collected on the handkerchief and said, "This is what's gonna happen to your lungs when you grow up, if you smoke." And from that day I made the decision not to, and I never did smoke cigarettes. So I wish someone had done the same thing with me on alcohol!

They talked to us strongly about God and Christ. This was the thing that was taught which I chose to stray away from later, but I came back. The presence of God was so strong that even though there were the outside people who wanted to gamble, the church in my life really stuck to me. You really didn't have much of a choice, because there was great dedication to that. Kids had speeches to say, verses to learn—that kind of thing. That's an old tradition which some of the black kids would still do right now. God was a loving God, but being a kid I had trouble because I could not see Him, and I couldn't understand that spiritual thing. A spiritual thing is not something that you see. Kids would have those kinds of questions. But you could look at your mother and see her, hear her praying and then you'd look back at things you made it through, and kind of wonder—you know: Who's this? What is this God she's talking about here? You just kept being good. For God always did answer my mother's prayers. It may not have been as quickly as I would like, but it was on time.

My mother would always take me to church on Sunday—she insisted on us going to Sunday school. The Sunday school classes brought us together; we could see people, and I had a lot of cousins. It was just the shoes that made me uncomfortable. It was a Baptist church. My dad would seldom go near church unless something was going to take place afterward; then he would hang around with another group of people waiting outside. He never would go inside. I had a good relationship with the minister. He dealt with the kids on a one-on-one basis like he dealt with the grown parents. The Sunday school teachers were my cousins. Most of them were on my mother's side. My mother's family always pushed their kids to be teachers because that was the thing then for Negroes. My mother's brother, Reverend Oliver, lived about two or three blocks away, and he had a son my age. He was a preacher and all along he would take me to do things like fishing. He just sort of moved into being a role model after my father left for Houston.

We used to have Christmas and my people would always make us go to bed early on Christmas Eve so that Santa Claus could come. They would take me to a Christmas party at the school, and they'd have this guy playing Santa Claus. I thought he was the real Santa Claus, and the guy would just have me totally petrified. You had to be there or you weren't going to get any toys. The last

Christmas before my mother decided to move to Houston, I went to bed early and I woke up in the night, and she and my sisters were putting the toys out. That was a total shock to me. It just killed the spirit of Christmas. There was no Santa Claus; it was only a joke. I was very disappointed.

We always looked forward to June 19 because that was the big day. That was the day supposedly that the slaves were freed. Actually, slavery ended several months earlier, but the plantation owners in Texas did not want their slaves to walk off and leave them with all the crops not finished. So they held this information back until June 19, then they told the blacks that slavery was ended. On June 19 my uncles would barbecue goats. But I enjoyed June 19 because there was a lot of pop, a lot of barbecue, cakes, and everybody cooked all this and brought it and you just ate. That was fun and you could kind of forget things.

White Bible   *Brown Bible*

Black Bible

$\mathcal{M}$y school was so small, some grades had to be split. The rooms had to be split. As little kids, we got a small room, but we always had to pass through the large rooms where the large kids were, so you could see this when you came in the front door. All different grade school kids were in the same building. During my last year at the country school, the teachers would always send me to pick up the mail. I'd have to go about two miles every mail day. I think that kind of deprived me of some of my studies, but I was the only one they could trust, and the people in the town knew me. As a black kid, you are careful, courteous, and you have to know how to play your game and be respectful or you might get yourself hanged. The other boys were jealous of me getting the mail and they called me names. They called me "One-Gone" because I didn't have time to chase the girls or play like they did. "One-Gone" means that you haven't got any desire anymore for girls—that you lost one of your testicles.

Another thing that made me different from them is they played basketball, football, baseball, and all those things. I really didn't like basketball at that time; I thought girls played it most and seemed to be good at it. I wasn't too fond of football. I sort of thought baseball would be good but I never did go out for it because my interest was high jumping. The principal of my school, New Hope, picked me as being the best high jumper. I trained hard and didn't do anything else but train, even while all the other kids were playing or having fun.

Once a year there was a relay seven miles from our town, where different schools would compete. I felt pretty good about myself, and felt like I was going to win. I had this hopeful feeling that went right on down to the final day. I went to school and we were all ready to go and we sat and waited and waited. No bus came. The principal kept telling me it was all right. I kept falling deeper and deeper into disappointment. Then someone came to the school and talked to the principal. He told me he wanted to apologize. The bus was not going to take us to the relay. The white kids had something else to do, so they got the bus and we didn't. That shot all the work that I had done, all the hope that I had—the whole thing just went down the drain. I listen to people talk about kids and the Olympics, and I understand what they're talking about—how the kids work so hard and come up to a point and then the event is canceled. But when the event is canceled, everybody sympathizes with the kids. But nobody sympathized with me. It was a battle I fought all by myself. I had nobody to go to (although I had no idea then what kinds of pressures the principal was under).

I'm sure the principal felt belittled. The strangest twist with him was later on, after I was down in Houston in school and working nights. During the summer when school got out, the principal came to where I was working and he had to take a job bussing dishes with me because he didn't have any money. They weren't paying him enough money, so during the vacation time he hadn't any money saved up, and he had to find work to survive. He was hired and I was told to train him. I couldn't figure whether to dislike him—it wasn't really his fault—but if he had just found something better. He reminded me of the situation, and he was embarrassed.

My dolly true dolly true dolly true

Rosary Beads

I n 1942 or 1943 my dad decided to pick up stakes and go to Houston to find other work. My oldest brother had been living there with my grandmother, helping support us on the money he earned being in the army. I didn't see him for four years. When my mom got ready to move, I hesitated and questioned it: Is it any different there than it is here? The best explanation I could get was, "Well, you can get a job, and you can get some more things."

For a kid, there wasn't any difference from the country to the city. I could see blacks laughing when they didn't want to laugh; when there was a joke told about them, they had to laugh. It got to the point that I didn't want to laugh, so I didn't go! I refused. I guess I was in the eighth grade. I objected so highly to going to Houston that my aunt Liza let me stay with her for another semester. I had heard people talk about the north and how it was better, and I think that struck me, that I wanted to get there instead of here because how could it be any better from Goodrich to Houston? How could 60 miles be any different?

You know, I think that God had reins on me, because all the traumatic things that were happening to me were enough to send me a little off-cuckoo. What had set me to believe was in spite of all this happening, I thought, "I'm gonna make it, because there has to be something better than this somewhere."

I had my first drink when I was twelve, just before I moved to Houston, just before my dad left. We had some beer, and he thought I would not like it, sort of like the teacher did with cigarettes. He had good intentions and he wanted me to taste it so I wouldn't want it. Strangely enough, I liked the taste, and I drank some more, and then I went home and picked a fight with my sister. It made me feel "upps!" You know, like walking on a cloud.

Following this I moved to Houston. I was entering the ninth grade and had to work. My father's brother, Uncle Sunboy, had a cafe there and almost worked me to death. The cafe was on Lyons Avenue. The area was so bad that they changed the name of the street. The war was on then, and the people started calling the street Pearl Harbor. I remember when I would go round there and something was fixing to take place, the run-for-cover word was "Look out!" You'd run for cover and you would fall onto the ground because someone was shooting or stabbing. You were always uptight all the time there. On weekends, sirens started Friday evening and went through Sunday.

We had to split up. My mother didn't stay in that area because it was too bad. I think she stayed over near her brother. I just had my sisters there and a little boy I played with who lived in the building. A guy here in San Francisco who I met there, in that area, taught me how to ride a bicycle about that same time. I was trying to go to school and cope with what was in school, and on weekends I had to get up at five o'clock and go down to the cafe and work. I don't think my uncle was very nice because he didn't pay me anything. I grew up some resentments. When my father would come around, my uncle would sort of ignore paying me.

I didn't really have a hand to guide me, so therefore, I had to start thinking for myself. "How am I going to make it out of this?" It was an experience coming from the country to living in Houston. You had to learn how to survive with all the shootings and stabbings. It was like a war zone. You had to learn that when somebody hollered, "Look out!" you knew you'd better run and

23

get some cover somewhere, get down, get on the ground or sidewalk. So when you walked around there you always listened for that warning sound. You could never really be comfortable there on Pearl Harbor Street.

I remember a storefront where people used to come to gamble. It stayed open twenty-four hours. In Texas you couldn't sell liquor after midnight, but this place sold liquor after hours. Men would stand around outside throwing dice for nickels and dimes, but the big stuff was inside. People drove up in cars and were really dressed. Being kids, we weren't allowed to go in, but we'd watch the people going in and out, and knew something was going on. We could hear them talking about gambling: "Let's get a game going," or "The game's starting." I was always curious about what they were doing and I knew whatever it was it had to do with getting money. In our community gamblers and hustlers were outcasts, but it seemed that these guys had more money than the church folks had. I didn't know what was going on in there, but my curiosity and my desire to know made me forget the things that I had been been taught and warned about.

I wanted that stuff! I could see it and thoughts of when I'd get the right shoes and the pants would take hold. They used to wear what they called back then zoot suits—"drapes." Those suits were so big; the upper legs were so full but down at the ankle you had to squeeze your feet in to get into them. Then they had these big gold chains, and they'd swing them around. It was good material, good-looking stuff, and it was hot looking. It seemed like the gamblers always had money to spend. They would give me candy or something like that. In spite of all the fighting and stuff that went on around there you'd always find some nice guy who would throw a little something your way. During that time a nickel was a whole lot of money.

My uncle's brother, Schofield, who we called Uncle Man, took up with this woman. She had killed several men already, and everybody was saying, "Why do you want to take up with a hooker?" He had no explanation for it. Nonetheless, she ended up killing him. She stabbed him because of something he said. He didn't bring her the money that he promised to bring. I don't think she was a falling down drunk. I think her game was to get as much money as she could off a guy. She would just get taken to jail and then turned loose again.

After that, another thing happened: I had a second- or third-cousin, one of the bad boys, the Jesse James of that little neighborhood. Everyone, even the police, was afraid of him because he wouldn't take anything off anyone. When the police wanted to arrest him for some things he had done, they sent word for him to come downtown. He said, "Why don't they come down and get me!" They were afraid to come and get him, so they talked his trusted friend into betraying him. The friend waited in his house until my cousin went to sleep, and then he carried out his guns, two 45's, and called the police. Then the police went in and shot and killed him while he was asleep.

*A*nother thing happened in the Deluxe Theater, which was several blocks away, where I would go and think it was safe. I was sitting in the movie and this man and his wife sat on the other side of me, and then some other man came in and sat on the woman's other side. As the movie was playing the woman suddenly jumped up and said, "You've got no business putting your hands under my dress!" The guy jumped up and ran out and the husband ran after him. I heard somebody say, "Oh, he stabbed him!" and everybody ran out. When I got out into the lobby, the guy was lying on the floor and the blood was just shooting up; he had been stabbed and died. Unfortunately, this was a common event.

Then in the same general area, they had this club called Crystal White. There were six brothers there. One was a very nice guy, living very well in the community—a typical good family man. The others were just gamblers, alcohol drinkers, and fast-life guys and they all ran together and were disliked. Four brothers were outside the club and the youngest went inside. He got into an argument with some of the guys who disliked him, and one shot him. Someone ran outside and told the other brothers, "Someone just shot your brother!" They came running in the door and they got shot one by one as they came in. All of them were shot. They were all buried together. It was a sad occasion. So the violence continued. It didn't go anyplace. Thirty-four years later, someone killed my uncle. He was still there, in the same place, running a little cafe, and somebody broke in to steal something and killed him. He was old.

I'd see my mother sometimes on weekends. She was not working; she had no skills. My younger sister, Jean, stuck with her and didn't get married until she was in her 40's. I didn't see my dad very much, because that was about the time he started to not be showing up at all. He was supposed to give my two sisters some money for support, and sometimes he'd show and sometimes he wouldn't. He would go to his job and then he would just slip on out the back door. It steadily got worse. He got a job at an iron factory. That was about the only thing he could do without having to read and write. I went to see him a few times after he took up with another lady, after my mom finally got fed up and said, "That's it." I went to see him around the time I was going away. He would just sit at home alone for hours. That's why it's not strange or odd for me to sit places alone, for hours, with my thoughts. I might be alone but I'm not really alone.

Hallowee

Aloha

Candle

Aloha

2 day

Blue Eyes

Honnolulu

2 date

gree

Candy

Hawy Eyes

27

I didn't have anything else to drink until I was fifteen. One thing I'd just say about the crooks in that area, they never offered kids any drink. They'd say, "Get outta here; get off the street." After getting up to fifteen years old, I was in high school and I had to go to work, so I got this little job downtown at a cafe called One-A-Meal. There were older people working there so I was the youngest one there. They would buy this wine called Ol' Abbey wine. Walgreen's Drugstore, adjacent to the cafe, sold that brand. These guys would ask, "Do you want a little nip?" so I'd take a little nip. It tasted pretty good, you know. From then on, that's when my drinking career really started.

I grew a mustache and looked older than I actually was, and in some places I could go and buy liquor, and they didn't question me that much. I had these favorite stores that I found, and I started to buy liquor for things like dances. Big bands would come into town—Lucky Millander and Lionel Hampton would be at the Civic Auditorium—and everybody would be down there, blacks and a few whites would come down. That started me on my drinking career. I was meeting other people still older than I was. So my little outlet was to dance or go to the wrestling matches.

That's when I started to kind of stray. I was still trying to hold up in school, and some drastic thing happened to me. The last year was so tough. I would have to get out of school at three o'clock and I was due to work from four to twelve. We had a study period in school and I couldn't get all my lessons done. Sometimes I'd have to hustle home and try to get my sister to do some things for me. I would have to go to work and didn't have time to study because the restaurant was so busy, and I had to come home and study. I'd just fall asleep on the bus. Sometimes the driver would let me ride all the way to the end of the line and come back to where I was living and then he'd wake me up and say, "Okay, it's time to get off." And I'd go home and then I'd do a little studying, but most of the studying I'd try to do at lunchtime. I was just barely making it through school.

I gave my paycheck to my mom. I saw that I just wasn't going to be able to make it. I was just too tired. I made a decision to drop out of school for a year. I talked to my mother about it and she said, "Are you sure you're going to finish?" I promised her that I would finish my last year.

Special Report dee 8/0,ans

*A*t sixteen, I started my restaurant work at 35 cents an hour. When I left four years later, I was making 50 cents an hour. During my time at this job and at my next job with a paint company, I met some very wild and sharp cats who were older than I. I was impressed with their street wisdom. I would listen a whole lot to whatever they were teaching me and then I would go and put my own twist on it. I had this big dream of what I was going to have that nobody else had. I never had any idea of stealing it; I was just going to outsmart somebody. Yet I didn't consider myself smart; I considered myself a survivor. You might say I was an independent follower. I was also a loner. When too many things are happening and I'm too entwined with people, it's like a war zone for me. I get relief from the chaos when I'm alone, but I'm not antisocial.

I never drank alone. I went out and did that. Alcohol became a sedative that made me feel a little bit at ease with this "war" going on around me. It also helped me relax more with the girls. I wasn't too successful with the girls, and I'm not sure I wanted to be. I was afraid that the hardships of my childhood would repeat themselves in an eventual marriage. I didn't want my kid to go through what I did growing up. As time went on, I just made the decision that marriage wasn't for me.

After not too much time I enrolled in night classes and finished high school. Toward the end of my school year I started working for another paint store. Jack's Paint was a small, family-type store that dealt in a variety of little things, and I thought that I'd enjoy the change. However, I soon regretted my move. There was a black guy working there whose name was Miles, and for some reason I never could figure out, he disliked me from Day One. He wasn't born in Texas; he was raised somewhere up north, and he looked down on me. I was a young kid and he was an older man, and he didn't want to teach me anything. He was supposed to train me but he really didn't want to show me anything or share any of the things he knew. His attitude was that I should have known everything by then and he talked about how stupid and dumb I was and that I never learned anything in school—as if school could teach me about paint. This was the first black guy whom I worked with who ever treated me in such an abusive and unfair way. I felt like I had been cast into hell. The up side was that it helped me become a survivor, because I had to figure out a system that would keep me going at that job despite some deep-seated resentment.

San Mateo
general

Huts of City

PART II

Manhood: Racism and Alcohol— Serious Drinking

*I*n one sense it was good news when I received my draft summons and I was able to leave that job. I was drafted on January 4, 1952. I was about twenty years old and had recently finished high school. There were about three hundred, more blacks than whites, down at the draft board on that particular day, and we all just sat there until around 3:00 PM. I'll never forget when that great big marine came out of this little door. The guy had to bend over to get out and he came to where we all were waiting, picked up the mike, and said, "I'm Lieutenant So-and-So and I need nineteen volunteers for the Marine Corps. Do I have any volunteers?" I think about five guys volunteered, so then he said, "Well, we have no more volunteers, so we'll have to pick the ones we're gonna have to take. So just relax and I'll be back with the names of the ones we picked."

When he returned a while later to announce the names, I was number seventeen on the list—just short of not making it. I'll never forget it. I felt so sick because all my buddies were gone. They went the other way. Among the nineteen of us there were more whites. I didn't know anybody, and on top of that, this other sergeant appeared and said, "I've got a surprise for you. You guys are gonna be able to spend one more night at home tonight, but first you gotta go out and pack the major's householdings because he's shipping off to Korea." So we had to go out and pack this major's family things and his wife's clothing and all this stuff, and then they let us go home that night.

The next morning, we reported to the train station. We had a stopover to wait for more troops in Flagstaff, Arizona. Boy, it was cold out there! It was snowing. I had seen snow before—a little fell in the country, but not that much. This was a very cold winter, and when we got off the train, snow was all we could see. We were still wearing our civilian clothes and I had this little old short topcoat which was kind of heavy and helped me a whole lot. I threw it away when I got to San Diego, my new home.

Serious boot camp began in San Diego and it was obvious that we were getting ready to go into action, bound for Korea. That's when I first got baptized. One of the navy chaplains baptized me at the Baptist church downtown. I was getting ready to go into action, so I wanted to have the protection of the church. I had never really gotten baptized when I was in the country, even though I was made to go to church and trained in the faith. I think it was considered a choice that one would make as a grownup.

Boot camp was strenuous, tough training that was transforming boys into men. The guys who couldn't make it fell out. Some of them got sick; some of them just took off over the hill. During the nine weeks of boot camp there was no drinking going on and no sight of any ladies.

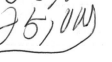

A's our nine weeks neared completion, we were certain that we were headed for Camp Pendleton and then Korea. Then a strange thing happened: Platoon 67 was pulled out and they told us we were going to Seattle. And we thought, "Seattle?" One guy had heard a story about mistreatment of prisoners in the brig. Walter Winchell had even gotten involved. He was supposed to have said that if you had a son in Korea, write him a letter, but if you have a son in the brig in Seattle, send him a prayer. All of a sudden, we were on a rackety airplane destined for Seattle, to replace the guys who were in charge of the brig there, who were being shipped off to Korea. I was spitting blood when we got there!

By this time, President Truman had integrated all the services, and that was an experience! Some of the white guys were hostile. I remember one white kid confessed one night when we were all sitting together, " All this time, I though we guys were a little better than you guys." I asked him what made him change his mind and he hesitantly replied, "I split up with my girlfriend back home because she wanted to help this black lady whose car had broken down. I refused to help the lady and told her to get out of the car. That's bothering me now." In response to his confession, I said, "You guys are no different from what we are." That was the first time I had that kind of conversation with a white guy, and I admired his sincerity. We became close and he eventually went to Korea. I don't know what happened to him. He was from one of the little suburbs in Houston.

In Seattle things were tough, and the tougher things got, the closer it brought most of us. You came to the realization that you would need to depend on one another in battle. We were pretty jumpy and edgy most of the time because you never knew when your name was coming up to be sent to Korea. It was like playing cards. As the guys were getting bumped off in Korea, they would send an order out for replacements from our group. I would always think back to Houston when my name came up as number seventeen, and I'd say, "Oh God, is this going to be another one of those things?" On any given day, someone out of our unit was being ordered to Korea. We had this big bulletin board. If a guy got killed, they'd paste a clipping from his hometown up on the bulletin board. These were guys whom we all knew, so it was very shocking to read about their deaths on the battlefield.

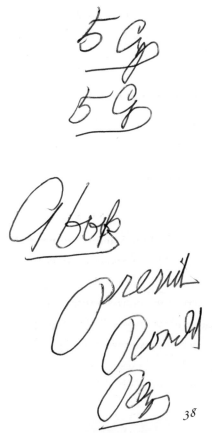

One Cake

Even worse than that, the most mind-boggling thing about guarding the brig in Seattle was the possibility that you might end up shooting a fellow American under orders. Guys coming back from Korea would make a stopover and be called to take positions as guards. A lot of these guys couldn't handle the duty with this possible consequence and decided they'd rather go back to Korea. They'd go out and get into a fight or something in order to get shipped out. This actually gave the rest of us the chance to stay there as long as we kept our eyes open and stayed clean. There was this one particular person whose name was Frank, who I suppose got killed over there because I never saw him again. He had hocked his ring. He looked at me when he got ready to leave and said, "I feel I can trust in you. Will you please go down to the pawnshop and get my ring out and keep it until I come back?" It was a small diamond ring, real stuff, and it cost me 15 bucks to get it out. From that day to this day I still have his ring waiting for him, and he can have it for 15 bucks. But I never saw him again.

By the time I got to Seattle, I was the only black man in my outfit. I had a black friend who covered the brig on another shift, and he and I became pretty close buddies. I asked my sergeant if I could transfer over to this guy's duty station so that we could go places on our day off and that sort of thing. The sergeant snapped, "No. I won't do that. It's too hard as it is—all this segregation stuff, then you come asking me a thing like that. I don't want you over there. I don't want all you black guys together. I want you all over the place. Hear?" I was a little upset when he first said this;

after all, I wasn't trying to get away from the whites. Then I understood where he was coming from. Actually, the white guys had a tougher time breaking in than the black fellas because we were used to taking orders. I'd been saying, "Yes sir" all my life.

The sergeant who wouldn't transfer me to my friend's unit was actually the best guy we had there. Sergeant Moses and I had many long talks. He was real good. He knew how to handle men. But then they sent this little lieutenant in from Texas, and boy, he just didn't like black folk. He was so bad that the white guys got fed up with him. I had a bad experience with him.

*D*uring my shift, the corporal would send us around 9:00 at night to the mess hall to pick up some milk and sandwiches. We did this all the time and it was expected that we would come each night to pick up our food. On one particular night, a navy lieutenant came in and said, "What are you doing in the box?" He obviously saw me coming out of the refrigerator. I told him that I had come to pick up the milk and rations. He demanded to know who told me to go into the box, and I said, "The cook told me to go in and get the milk while we were waiting on the sandwiches." He said, "You're not supposed to be in that box." I told him that I was given orders by my corporal to come over and pick up the food. Meanwhile, the cook—who was on some kind of probation—told the lieutenant that he did not tell me to go get the milk. So this lieutenant called the little marine lieutenant from Texas and all of a sudden, at 3:00 in the morning, I was arrested for stealing milk. My shift was over and I had just gotten to sleep when I saw this guard hanging over me saying, "Lieutenant Hollins's got us arresting you." They stripped my gun and told me that I was under house arrest and that I would see the major in the morning. I was scared to death. I was totally by myself. Nobody knew anything. I had to go see the major.

Early the next day, the guards escorted me over to the major. Instead of doing one of those numbers to me with the gun, chasing me, they escorted me. Chasing prisoners with our guns was "the thing to do" when you moved them from one place to another. And if a guy was kicked out of the service, you literally booted him out of the front gate. Anyway, there I was before the major and this lieutenant from Texas, and it was my word against his. He went through this whole ritual. The major listened to him and then looked up and said, "Lieutenant Hollins, who sent the man over there in the first place?" Hollins replied that the corporal on duty had given me the order. The major told Hollins to bring in the corporal, who told the lieutenant that I was following orders, that picking up food had been going on for years, and that he should not have brought me up on charges for following orders. I could not stop thanking the major; I was so happy and grateful!

Hour 8
Merge Coffee

My girlfriend and I broke up long before I got out of the service. I didn't have any money to chase anybody, so I spent a lot of my spare time reading. There was also the radio, when I could get it before anyone else did. I enjoyed listening to a guy who used to talk about Norman Vincent Peale-type stuff. I don't know how deep I was into it, but it got me thinking about my future: What kind of job will I get? How much money will I be able to make? When I get back to Houston, will it be different? I always assumed I'd have to go back to Houston to see how things were with my mother. As far as a job and money, I was never an A student but I had a great gift of common logic, which got me through a whole lot of things. I was counting on this to help me survive. By the time I was 23, I was beginning to realize that I could learn just about anything if I got the chance. Oh, I'd end up doing it my way, but I'd get to the same place as the other guy. So I was confident that I could learn a job well enough to move up and advance in position and pay. I wasn't concerned how I started—whether pushing a broom, cleaning a toilet—I knew I had the winning combination of desire to learn and willingness to do whatever I had to do to get started. I think all this self-knowledge solidified for me while I was in the marines.

After being two years in an integrated situation, I was angry to return to Houston and find racism still going strong. I thought there was a great deal of injustice in a lot of things. I was angry because I felt my life had been on the line in the service. My Daddy went to World War I, my brother to World War II, gone for four years from my life. And here I am back in Houston, finding the same mess as when I left! I didn't have my comrades from the service to talk to about it, but I did talk to some of the other guys around who had been in the military. I dealt with guys who were older all the time because I felt I got a lot of wisdom from my conversations with them.

I got out of the service in January 1954 and almost immediately found out about a two-year course in photography that was being given at Texas Southern University. I had developed an interest in photographic skills. I went right to the Veterans Administration because I didn't have any money, and I was able to enroll under the G.I. Bill. I became the assistant photographer for the instructor and therefore had access to a lot of equipment. People got to know me and I started making a little money. A student friend and I set up a darkroom together, and contacts came through the school.

I think in 1956 is where and when serious drinking came into the picture (no pun intended). I knew most of the faculty and the kids. I was like a brother at all the frat parties and gatherings. I also got pretty good in the wedding field, another time when people would invite me for drinks.

I broke into commercial stuff a little bit by doing the yearly state fair at Dallas for the school newspaper. I earned a little reputation when the city papers would pick up some shots from the school newspaper. These shots belonged to the school, but I got my own cards made and started shooting commercial pictures on my own.

*A*round that time, I went downtown and applied for a job at United Gas Company. The guy looked at me, laughed, and said, "Gee, these guys have been here some twenty-odd years and I don't think they're ever gonna quit now." I told him I was just trying and would take whatever he had open. We chatted and I told him I had just gotten out of the Marine Corps. He said, "Okay. Fill out the application and if anything comes up, I'll call you." About three weeks later, something came up. They needed some students to run the elevators at night. So he hired me and asked if I had a buddy over at school looking for work, since he wanted two people.

It worked out real good with the two of us because we could cover for each other if one of us had something to do. I could even study there and it didn't really interfere with my photography. We'd work ten hours for four days and then be off for three days. We had more money than the other kids because we were working full-time. We'd show up at the Grill, a bar right across the campus, and this is where we'd spend our money. Back then you brought your own liquor into the club and you had to buy the set-up, like ice and milk. The favorite drink was VAT 69 and White Horse scotch whiskey. You'd mix milk with it and this is the way we'd entice the girls to come over for some drinks. The money we were making allowed us to go out and do some wheeling and dealing, and we got to know a whole lot of people. You always invited folks over for a drink and got invited back in return. So it started a pattern for drinking. I never can remember falling down drunk; nothing more than having a little funny feeling. And I didn't drink again until the next weekend when I went to another one of these clubs.

I now realize that social drinking is the first step to alcohol addiction. It borrows from the future, then takes it away (it's cunning and baffling). The Bible states in Proverbs 20:1, "That wine is a mocker, strong drink is raging, and whosoever is deceived thereby is not wise."

I was disappointed that the photography course was only for two years. We got a lot of basic stuff but we didn't have any way to specialize. I talked often with my instructor. We were very close; as a matter of fact, when I go to Houston each year, I always visit with him. Before he retired, I'd go over to the college and we'd sit down and talk for an hour about what had been happening and where all the guys had gone. I always had a good feeling talking to him and it was very nice because he was always very happy to hear from me. That man was really an inspiration for young guys just out of the service. He always took a lot of time with us. One time he said, "You know, if you want to go further in this field, you're going to have to go somewhere else, because you aren't gonna get it here. You might try the University of Houston, but you know what's going on over there." Blacks were not accepted at Houston at that time. So I started to write to a couple of big schools, New York Institute, and Brooks Institute in Santa Barbara—which I finally attended.

As a photographer at Texas Southern University (TSU), I covered sports events, and started to have a little following. Women seemed to be attracted to anything that related to sports, and I ended up having the time of my life. I bought my first car at the time. I couldn't even drive the thing! A friend of mine insisted that I drive him and his girlfriend around all night until I got the hang of it. To summarize the state of my life at that time: I was drinking but it wasn't a problem. I was kind of a celebrity among my peers because of the photography and I had a chance to observe many facets of college life in the sports, academic, and political arenas. On top of all that, my social life was very full and I had a great mentor. I had some good friendships, like the one with the older guy at the store who was helping me out. I was still helping my mom out. I was living with her at the time. In short, it was a very nice life.

About segregation back then: They were testing blacks for the police department and this guy, Walter was his last name, was very bright. He was smart enough to pass their stiff exam and he became their first black policeman. One day he was on his way home and there was a white guy at the bus stop who was drunk and meddling with this black lady, snatching at her while cursing and ridiculing her, calling her names the whole time. Walter arrested the guy and took him over to the jail. Would you believe it, they put Walter, the policeman, in jail and turned the white guy loose instead! They said there was a law there that blacks couldn't arrest whites. That was a law! I couldn't stop laughing. So the guys at school had to scramble down and bail the guy out. We all just donated; everybody chipped in. We were hoping to save his reputation.

While living in Houston those two years, I really didn't have any white friends to speak of. The guys who were in the service with me all went different ways. In Houston, there were definite black and white areas and you just kind of stayed with your own where you were comfortable. I did know some white people, good people, but the law said you weren't even supposed to go into their house and things like that—not to mention that the neighbors didn't approve of this kind of thing. But I did befriend this one guy, an older man with a family. We worked at the store together.

*T*his was right around the time of Brown vs. the Board of Education. We younger people had a "wait and see" attitude about the case. We were looking for that spark of hope, and Thurgood Marshall seemed to have the magic touch for that kind of thing at that particular time. He worked for the NAACP—of which I was a member—at the time he argued this case. He was a great inspiration to the students at Texas Southern. He took the case all the way to the Supreme Court and the Court declared the "separate but equal" laws were unconstitutional. We had a great speech debating team of which (Senator) Barbara Jordan was a member, as was Jefferson Andrew, who became a federal judge. Then there were the Key brothers, Bud and Hayman, who both became attorneys.

As assistant photographer, I won a few certificates for taking pictures of groups and of some of the bright stars on the debating team. TSU was small but it was producing good people. It was originally called Houston Negro College until a Dr. Lanier came from Africa and formed TSU. He eventually was dismissed because he didn't play politics with the financial contributors who, in fact, controlled the college.

TSU became a jumping-off point for civil rights activism after Brown vs. the Board of Education, but the focus was more local than national, confined to Houston. We were involved in picketing, rallies, and demonstrations—many of them aimed at a wealthy white man on the board of directors who had political pull. As assistant photographer at all these events, I was getting a political education. Just before I left I was offered a job on a black paper, the Houston Informer. The deal died, however, because the salary was very low and the cost very high, especially since I would have to give up my schooling.

Segregation had such a far-reaching impact. If I could have gone five blocks over to the University of Houston and finished my photography I'd probably still be there contributing something good to the city. However, I had to pack up my bags and go to a strange place—Santa Barbara, California, to attend Brooks Institute—where I didn't know a soul, and start all over again. But I didn't let it defeat me; I did what I had to do. As for my drinking, it was considered the mark of a man in the black neighborhoods: "You're not a man if you can't take your liquor." You never heard anything about how you might become addicted. I had a great girl back then, when I was twenty-four, and I lost her because my drinking came between us. I'm sure we would have gotten married. But she saw no future.

O n January 1, 1957, I got into my car and headed for Santa Barbara. My brother-in-law drove out with me. He was going to San Francisco so he drove as far as Santa Barbara, and then I was on my own. It was really foggy, both in weather and in feelings. I didn't know a soul; I couldn't see a foot in front of me, and I was way up in the mountains looking for the school. I had no idea where I was. I was lost in more ways than one! I went to someone's house for help and they called the school.

The school sent someone in a van to lead me there. They had arranged a place for me with this black lady, Meryl. We hit it off pretty good. I rented a room from her for most of the time I was there. It was a double and my roommate was a guy from New Jersey. We hung out with another guy named Bob (he's an attorney now here in San Francisco) and with Grace Bumbrey, the opera star. She could really sing and touch your heart. She attended the Music Academy in Santa Barbara. On Sundays the black kids would all meet at her girlfriend Freddie's house, and she would put on this little singing show for us. After she became famous, she didn't recognize me anymore.

There were three hundred students at Brooks, and only four or five of us were black. The white guys had the money for college, so they were in the majority. I didn't have any money, so I got a job at a bar, the Tyro Club, to supplement my GI Bill. I would help the bartender clean and straighten up and reload his boxes with beer, and while setting up we'd drink half the beer the owner had stocked. When she discovered the amount of beer we had consumed, she was in disbelief! My drinking was definitely increasing at this time, maybe due to the new pressures or even grief over what I had to sacrifice to go there. It was serving as a combination of gratification and anesthetic to kill some of the pain.

Being poor just added more misery because it prevented me from keeping up with the others. For example, my instructor, Mr. Lawson, was always asking me to experiment with chemicals in developing, as the other students were doing. I had to tell him time and again that I only had money to survive and not to experiment. It was degrading to always have to borrow and beg equipment for special assignments. There was this one guy who had everything, including a big heart, and I was always borrowing from him. I felt I was imposing on his good nature.

PART III

Northern Brand of Racism:
Sinking Deeper

*I*n 1957 Santa Barbara was also the first chance I had, outside of the service, to experience northern attitudes about race. There was one particular man and his wife who ran a distilled water company. I was the only black and I never did find out what he or his foreman expected of me, but whatever it was, I never could fit the bill. The only friendly person was the secretary. She was the only one who spoke to me decently. The foreman would repeatedly tell me, "I don't know why they've got you around here; we don't need you anyway." Finally, he just told me, "Man, don't come back. We don't need you," and I could feel that! I was fired over an incident with a water truck which was exaggerated for the purpose of covering up their real reason for firing me: I was black.

This make-believe stuff was racism and segregation, northern style. If it had been in the south, there would be no punches pulled. If the guy didn't like you he'd say, "I don't want no Negroes around. I don't like Negroes." I could deal with this direct approach better in some ways because at least I'm not wondering what did I do wrong personally that I deserved to be fired. Racism is much more subtle in the north, and it feels like a personal attack. For example, I'll be talking to someone. A second white person will approach us, and looking right through me, will address himself to the white guy as if I'm not even there. That's the subtle stuff that you see.

I have to say that I didn't really experience this subtle treatment with the instructors at school in Santa Barbara. They were pretty fair and even-handed. But as soon as I got out of the classroom, it was there! It was the look that I got when I went into a restaurant. You know, when you come in, everybody seems to be so jolly, everything's going on—and then all of a sudden, you show up and they look up and see you and it's quiet. They seem surprised that you dared walk in there. You feel guilty before proven. So you just get out of there.

Back in school I had to figure out how to find who the good guys were and stick with them. Therefore, I didn't accumulate a whole lot of friends. I had three guys I was close to in school, and I felt like I was a liability on them since I went to them only every time I had to borrow something for filming.

More *More*

I was not that interested in commercial photography, shooting skylights, buildings, bridges. I wanted to specialize in portraiture. There were only white models. Finally, I brought a black model up to the school. I was the only black guy in the class and the only one who got an A on that assignment, because I knew that white reflects light and black absorbs it. So all you had to do was give her more light. The white guys had to keep reshooting because they kept coming up with totally black pictures. Anyway, the whole school only had five black Americans and one black African. And as I said before, I was far more comfortable with whites from the south than those from the north. I still feel uncomfortable with the guys from the north—I can't read where they're coming from. But the Southerners seem to shoot straight from the belt. Even today when I go back to Houston, I feel I am greeted better there than I am here. Of course there's the other, too! Some places still give me that strange look when I walk in, like they expect me to rob them or something.

As I mentioned, during my years in Santa Barbara, my drinking increased. I was full of self pity and rationalization and was looking for some immediate relief from some of the pressure at school. I constantly thought about how I was going to make my next dollar to pay my rent. The GI Bill was not giving me enough money. I had a hard time surviving. I used booze to ease my mind and my tension. But I never realized I had any problem, because I could drink and then stop and stay away from it for four or five days and then go back and have some more booze on the weekend. And I didn't really get drunk, just hung over, but it wasn't really a lasting thing. I don't even remember having any blackouts. I was just having a good old time. Then you went home and went to bed and did whatever—school or job—you had to do the next day. I actually rationalized that the booze was helping me by releasing my tension.

After graduation, I went to work at the Clift Hotel in San Francisco, which my boss at the Biltmore Hotel in Santa Barbara also ran. My first job there was as a linen man. It was a very heavy, strenuous job, loading and reloading linen and wheeling it around to all the different floors. Fortunately for me—or so I thought—there was a guy named Tim doing a lot of commercial work, and I spoke with him frequently about how I desired a job in the photography field. I was under the impression that Tim might eventually have an opening for me. Then a white kid started working at the hotel who was also interested in photography. All of a sudden, this kid announced to me that Tim was giving him a job. That really set me back. I was really disappointed that racism had once again entered the picture, which made me resentful.

Ten Community

I proceeded then to go out and seek jobs at other places and I had no luck. I didn't know that jobs were so controlled in the photographic field. It seemed like a family affair. If you didn't know the right people in the family, then you didn't get a job. I applied at a photography company for any job available and I caught the guy throwing my application in the garbage. That made me feel desperate so after that incident, I went out after any job I could find. The state had an opening for a janitor and in 1959 I started work.

At the same time, I was doing some freelance photography, and I met up with this black photographer in the city who eventually hired me to work at his studio. But I ended up becoming very good friends with the guy I was supposed to replace, and so we both quit and started club-hopping as freelancers. We'd go right into the nightclub or the dance, shoot our pictures, and then race to a darkroom in the city, then back to the event because the patrons wanted their pictures that very night. By the next morning, after the alcohol wore off, they wouldn't be interested and you'd be stuck with the pictures.

The incident with Tim felt like racism and I used booze to release myself since I didn't have anybody to talk to. When I applied to work with the city they told me I was overqualified, and that felt like racism as well. I had a whole life, a whole history of this stuff popping out at me. But I'm not a guy who chases after folks when these things happen. It's a waste of my time because it only upsets me and gets me in worse shape than I am already, so I tend to assume something else. I just move on.

But I kept asking myself, how long do I have to go through this stuff? When do I get past it? After all, I had left one state because of this stuff and here I come to another state and I have to go through the same thing! How far do you have to keep running? The injustice of it all started me to have an interest in politics—who was running and what the guy's record was about. I was a big supporter of the Burton boys—I felt their ideas fit closer to what I was thinking than any one else's.

Now, drinking can take the edge off any interest, including politics. I always felt that a few drinks would settle me down, help me to think clearly. Of course, the opposite always happens. Everything just seems to sort of subside and goes away. And the next day you're hung over and all your effort goes into getting yourself to work. That was very important to me. I didn't want to go to work drunk. In the field of photography you're around people who are drinking all the time, so it's open season! And again, the difficulty in finding a job helped the drinking along as well.

I felt that white folks were almost shocked that a black man came in and wanted to take their pictures. I always left room for that resistance by asking first if they had a job I could do in the darkroom. Because I knew some guy was not gonna let me step into his studio and start shooting pictures of white people. But I wanted a job in the field of photography. So logically, if I could get my foot in the door, I might eventually move up whenever something might open. I never worried about starting at the top. I'd start at the bottom and work my way up when the boss became impressed with my work. As I said, in Santa Barbara we only had one black model, and I knew exactly what I was doing. So I was shooting pictures of whites all the time. I was very confident that I would move up. And most new photographers would be looking for the same "foot-in-the-door" kind of position.

This one black man was the leading person in the field of photography in San Francisco, so that's where I went. As I said, it was a tremendous advantage that I was used to lighting people of all different skin tones. Also, since color is a serious issue in photography, it would be an area where racism would be most blatant, because photographs concentrate on people's skin. With all this in mind, the photography field was a lonely place for a black guy, and alcohol really started to become a companion to me. But it was only borrowing from the future, which eventually it took away.

When my friend and I had walked out on that guy, he started to run me down, saying, "I don't think Curtis is smart enough to make it." It reminded me of the guy in Houston who talked about me so badly before I went into the service. Yet here was a black guy doing the same. But what he was really angry about was that we were affecting his business. We were taking some business away from him. He had the only legit black studio in San Francisco, right on Fillmore in the heart of the Western Addition, which was predominantly a black area. I lived there myself. Anyway, once this guy told me that I was in and my new friend would soon be out, I said to myself, "I won't let this happen." So as I said, I told my friend and we had a few drinks and talked about it and we decided we could do about as good on our own. And of course the two of us got to be close drinking buddies, so I was drinking, working two jobs, chasing women, getting very little sleep, and always looking to make more money!

*O*f course, I blew a lot of money at the clubs, getting in to the people, setting up the table, and buying the booze. Nightclub people did not provide the solid base of friendship that I needed—they were here today and gone tomorrow. Booze continuously watered down my religion. I started to lose my roots at this turn in my life.

Around winter of 1961 business started to fall because there were so many people moving into the photographic field. Everywhere you'd turn there was someone with a camera. Photography was becoming too much hard work and too little money. So I decided to move on to something else. One night at a bar, while I was soothing my brain with alcohol, I met this guy sitting there with a big roll of money, buying drinks for everybody, and I thought, "Gee!" I sat right down beside him and started asking him where he got all his money. He said, "Well, I own my own barbershop business and you can make lots of money doing that!" And I said, "Boy, I think I want to be a barber." Just like that—boom!

The following Monday I went down to Moler's Barber College on Fourth Street and enrolled. I worked at night and completed the college during the day. Next I had to go before the state board and take the apprentice test, which I passed. Yet in order to own my own shop, I still had to get my master's license (this came as a surprise to me). So I first had to do eighteen months of apprenticeship under another barber before I could take my master's license test. My first job didn't amount to much. I was working for a black barber on Fillmore Street, but when customers came in he would immediately hog them all and leave me sitting there. I couldn't make any money and I had to move. I found a lady-owned shop on McAllister and Fillmore, and there I worked with a lady barber who taught me everything I needed to know about the art and skill of barbering. In fact, she's still cutting my hair!

I had this friend from barber school and we decided it was time to open a shop. We bought a shop on Third Street but then a new owner came in and threw us out. He had other plans even though he had promised not to kick us out when I conferred with him beforehand. "Oh no, you'll be there," he said. But as soon as the deal went through he changed his mind and we were out. That guy pulling what he did on me was a big shock. It took a lot of booze to get through it. Unexpected letdowns always seemed to get to me in a big way. You never get used to it.

I was always on the move. Even with jobs, I was always looking for the next better place. I left the state when I found out that the city was paying more money to push a broom. Meanwhile, soon after that guy kicked us out of the first shop, we found another one right off Third Street on Oakdale, which stood two blocks away from where we were originally. It worked well for me because I worked for the city at the zoo in the day and I changed the barbering hours till evening. But of course, when customers came in the evening, they wanted to have a drink with you, so there was always a reason for the booze.

My barbershop hours allowed for boozing before work and in-between. I could still camouflage the alcohol with gum or gargling or something like that or so I thought; it hadn't gotten to the point where I was stumbling around and missing work. After work sometimes, I'd stop by a bar or liquor store and make some runs, see what the girls were doing out there. And then there were the after-hours places that you could sneak into. My friend and I had moved from Fillmore to Precita at Mission. We'd drink quite a bit at the house because we always had company and so we kept booze. I drank in between my barbershop job and state job. Sometimes I drank before the barbershop job, and after went out clubbing or drank at the house. The amount of my drinking was accelerating, but I felt that drinking wasn't a problem! I began to feel that a shot or two gave me more energy and kept me moving. Business went very well but my partner wasn't satisfied with it, so he decided to go back to sea (he was a seaman). But I was able to handle the whole thing by myself. Of course, my drinking increased on a daily basis because that was my energy, that kept me going and feeling good when I got to the shop.

*I*n the midst of working, barbering, and heavy drinking, I met a lady at the shop whose son's hair I used to cut. We conceived a daughter, who is now in her thirties. I saw her until she was about three years old, and then I didn't see her for about ten years. At that particular time, this woman and I would have gotten married, but she didn't have her divorce, so that didn't happen. As time passed, contact between us was lost and she eventually got married again. When my daughter was thirteen, she decided she wanted to meet me. Her mother called to inform me of her request and I sent her the plane fare. It was a very strange feeling because I really didn't know what she looked like from when she was a baby. She had a picture of me so she touched me at the airport and said, "I think you're my dad." It was truly a shocking experience. My daughter and I are very close now. I feel very sad that she went through all her young life without having me around, but I'm trying to make amends to her.

After my daughter's mother, while I still had the barbershop, there was another lady in my life. She was white. That relationship put me in touch with big-time prejudice. We were together two or three years. Finally we both got tired of the hassles that we always had to go through. If it wasn't a hassle from the whites, it was a hassle from the blacks! There was always something. There were no major hassles, but very irritating occurrences, such as we'd go out someplace, a restaurant or a club, and some half-drunk guy would be sitting behind us blowing smoke down our backs. And if it wasn't that, people would be staring at us because there weren't many mixed relationships in the city at that time. Then we were sort of fenced in because we could only interact with that little circle of people who had open minds to this kind of relationship. The interesting thing was that there was no difference in the intensity of harassment, regardless of whether it was coming from the white community or the black community. It helped some that she lived in a mixed neighborhood, not an area where it was totally white. But most places that we went together were frequented by whites, such as the theater or the jazz clubs. The blacks were more open in their hostility; they would glare at us and mock us with jokes. So we always had to challenge somebody or something, like, "You don't do things like that to a lady." We could never relax. Fortunately, I never got into a physical fight. It was just mental warfare that never let up.

*T*he Small Business Administration was not letting many blacks have loans. A friend of mine, who was an attorney, approached me about going into partnership with him in a liquor store. I checked it out and talked to the person who owned the store. He was selling out because more and more blacks were moving in and he wanted to relocate and let some black person have the store.

I borrowed some thousands from my sister and we applied for a small business loan. We negotiated with the suppliers and had everything set. Then one day I got a call from my friend who said the deal was off. The Small Business Administration had turned us down. I said, "Turned us down! For what?" At that time, I had a clean record. I couldn't figure out what went wrong. The excuse they gave was that since I was single, it was too much of a risk (even though he was married). I was in disbelief! "Do you mean after going through all of these problems to get the cash, to buy the license and everything else now, they're turning us down? Oh, my Lord!" I decided it must have been racism.

I looked upon my drinking at that time as a normal thing to do because that's what I had been doing for a long time. I didn't see any problem with it, although others may have seen it as a problem. Some would ask me, "How can you drink so much?" But nobody ever offered a solution as to what I should do about it, or even suggested that there was something that could be done. So I presumed that it was all right because everybody else was drinking. And then when I went to the barbershop, whether it was morning or evening, there was some customer waiting on me who had just gotten paid the night before and so they always had the booze, and to keep the customers happy I had a highball with them. Why not? The drinking kept progressing but at that time I thought of it as social drinking, even though I "social drank" every night and quite a few mornings. It's strange how when you start off drinking, you think you can handle it; you are convinced that you can control it. And what made it seem even more harmless is that I didn't have heavy hangovers and I wasn't blacking out . . . yet.

Around the time I broke up with Mary, I was restless about the barbershop. I started working for Muni in 1968. I still owned the shop but it was fading, plus at that time it was becoming increasingly difficult to run the place. Training with Muni was tiring and the customers were getting on my case because I wasn't there when I should have been there. By the way, Muni probably had something to do with my girlfriend and me breaking up.

PART IV

Final Days of Darkness

1968 was also the year that Dr. King got murdered. It was quite a shock for me. It's sort of hard to explain the feelings that I had at that particular time. I really hit the sauce pretty heavy at that time. That was my tranquilizer for whatever was going on. I thought the man was doing a very good job; I admired him. I had records of him and I'd sit down and listen to those records and a lot of things that he was doing made a lot of sense. At that particular time, those who were involved in civil rights knew they were in danger of being killed while trying to affect the system. But somebody had to do it for any change to take place. I think what bothered me most was why this man had to put his life on the line for civil rights when blacks supposedly were given civil rights when the slaves were freed. It's like a replay of everything. As soon as he's dead and gone, somebody else has to take his place and continue fighting. I would like to think that civil rights would have happened when the slaves were freed. Martin Luther King was trying to get the people's attention. I don't know what motivates a guy to go into that kind of leadership. He has to be really dedicated.

King's murder provoked riots just six blocks from my barbershop. I just closed when things started brewing. One of my customers got shot in that rioting. The police came out and shot all the tires from under a Cadillac, and he was behind the car and got shot in his arms and legs. I could see him on TV hiding behind the Cadillac. I knew it was him. I didn't see him for awhile, but he finally got out of the hospital, on crutches. I was one of the fortunate ones. They broke up a lot of places and things around there. They didn't break up my shop.

Robert Kennedy's assassination had a strong effect on me as well. As I said before, it takes a special kind of person to be born to do that kind of thing, and I could imagine the fear they must go through every day. They must also get depressed. Just the little episodes that I was going through with the relationship that I had were depressing enough. And often I felt like we were in serious danger. I drank myself through Robert Kennedy's assassination as well as when Malcolm X was killed. I was using booze to keep my emotions in check. I drank by myself and with other people. We'd all sit down and drink and talk about what was happening. It was a very sad time. Actually, I felt a mixture of anger and sadness. For example, if there were about five people standing near you and one threw a rock and hit you on the head, then you're angry but you don't know who to fight because you don't know who threw the rock. That's the kind of feeling I had when Malcolm X was killed. I had read his books and at first I didn't quite understand where he was coming from, but as things went along, I began to understand. Alex Haley did a very good job on Malcolm X. When Malcolm went to Mecca he saw something else and began to change. I think the reason people feared him so much was because he told the truth. He was simply telling the truth. I really don't think he was advocating that people go out and start shooting. His real message was about history telling what history was all about. It was a statement about the struggle and suspicion between the blacks and whites which led them to fear for their lives at the hands of one another. He was, as with the other great leaders, trying to simply get people's attention. He wasn't planning to raise an army and begin attack. After all, he was just one guy.

The latter part of 1968 was mostly training and Muni. In February 1969 I was given my own run transporting passengers without the trainer present. Soon after, I had an accident with the Muni bus and hurt my back badly. As a matter of fact, I felt like I was paralyzed there for awhile. That was really a down part of my life. The day I had the accident, the inspector wanted to pull me off the line, but I ended up completing the shift. By the time my relief came I couldn't get out from under the driver's wheel. So he had to sort of drag me out of the seat. I was really frightened. When he got me out and to my car, I managed to drive out to San Francisco General Emergency.

They put me in a wheelchair and I had to wait a long time before I could see a doctor. Finally the nurse came and said she was taking me upstairs. She took me to a huge open area called Ward 44, which was filled with city employees, firemen, policemen, etc. After a very long wait, the doctor came out to look at me and ask me some questions. He prescribed some pills and told the nurse to send me home to get some rest. I told the nurse I couldn't move. I said, "I don't think I can walk." And she said, "Well, he said you're okay. Can you get up?" I told her I didn't know and asked her to help me out. I fell on the floor. They all ran out and put me on a stretcher and took me back to the ward, where I stayed in traction for seventeen days.

That was the real start of things going downhill. After seventeen days I was back on the job driving trolleys. The poles would slip off the wires and I would have to go out and jerk these ropes. It just wasn't working out. I'd throw my back out and I'd have to go back to the doctor. It was off and on, just like some of those back patients in Ward 44 had predicted when they told me their fearsome histories.

Some of the bosses began to say, "Well, you don't wanna work anyway. There's nothing really wrong with you." It was like being in limbo and I felt very alone. I was taking pretty strong pills but after a while, it seemed like the pills weren't really doing anything, so I thought, "Well, I'll take the pills in the daytime and maybe have a few highballs at night to settle me down some." I thought this was the thing that would do the trick. It did work for a while. But I was still back and forth between the doctor and work and finally I went to my union attorneys and appealed to them. It just made matters worse. This attorney decided to go to the state compensation board and they set up a fee schedule for me—$52.50 per week for 66 weeks so I could be off work to recuperate. Now how could I live on $52.50 a week? I was very angry. I called this attorney many times. I could hardly even get the $52.50. I had to call him up to get these people to send me out the money and all he ever said was, "Well, that was better than nothing."

Fighting with this and fighting with the injury and being treated in a kind of cruel way by people who accused me of not wanting to work—it all made me feel like I wasn't even a human being any more. I know racism was involved with this supervisor who kept telling me I was slacking off and I didn't really want to work. Other black drivers were having their share of problems, too. The judge was white, the lawyer was white, everybody was white. I did talk to one man who was the first black driver, and the employees themselves gave him some rough times.

During this time, drinking seemed to be the only thing that

helped me out in any way. I was starting to believe that it was solving some problems for me. I thought it was helping me deal with the pressure of trying to pay my bills on $52.50 a week. I was making too much for general assistance, and yet not enough to live on. I wasn't able to do any barbering because I had to stand and make different maneuvers that were physically impossible for me. So I had to figure out some kind of way I was going to make it through!

I started to watch pool shooters. And there was one particular black guy called Bill Bo from Mississippi, who played. He was a very good pool shooter. I watched that guy and admired him so I asked if he would teach me something about pool. He laughed at me, saying, "You don't even belong in this field!" But I made a deal with him. I said, "You know I don't have any money, but if you'd just practice with me I'll pay for the balls." He called me Lollipop shooter because I shot soft and this guy and his friends shot hard and long. They began to like me for some reason and so did the guy who ran the hall. I used to cut his hair so he watched out for me. Bill Bo taught me how to shoot but I could not emulate him. However, I did learn how to perfect cutting balls into the pockets. We call it "cut 'n' shoot." Instead of you shooting the ball straight the full distance, you cut it into the side pocket. I wouldn't shoot like they would shoot because I couldn't shoot that far, so I had to devise something else. And boy, I got good at that!

As a matter of fact, I got too good at it. I was so absorbed, I didn't realize what was happening. It seemed to me that if I had a few drinks it would make me shoot better. Guys were betting money on me. The other guys figured out that if I had too many drinks then I couldn't shoot. So they would buy me drinks and everybody would drink with me. Then as the money piled up, I would begin to lose my coordination and then I would lose the game and they would lose the pot on me. I can remember this one guy pulled a gun on me and said, " I should shoot you!" I couldn't figure out what he was talking about. He said, "You threw the game. You made me lose all my money!" I didn't throw the game;

I just lost it from intoxication. Some people talked him down and by the grace of God he didn't shoot me. Another time, some guy pulled a knife on me.

I wasn't a very good hustler myself, but when I won, these guys would share the pot with me and it always amazed me to make such pretty good easy money. After the game was over the owner would come up to me and say, "Here's the money you won on the game." I took the money to pay my bills and didn't ask too many questions.

When I finally got back to work, I was off and on the buses. Management finally decided to send me to do light duty. They sent me over to one of the mechanic shops where they repaired the buses. They had this open space which they drove the buses over. The mechanics walk down into this pit and can work underneath the bus. All this oil drops down into this hole from the bus and so they put sand down to soak it up. This sand has to be changed regularly. That's where I came in. The guy in charge says to me straight off, "I don't know why they sent you over here to me, but it's obvious that you don't want to work. If you don't work here I'm gonna send you back where you came from." So that was our starting-off point!

I made up my mind that I was gonna show this guy that I could work, man, regardless of what it takes. I'm gonna do the best I can. I had no idea he was going to tell me to clean out all those pits. I didn't even have anything to get it out with. So the car cleaners who clean all the trash off the buses had these big metal containers for trash that was being carried to the dumpster. So I took that thing and went down and got the shovel, and I put the sand into the metal container. What I had in mind was to stair-walk it up. I got almost to the top and the thing slipped off the steps and started to go back down. I couldn't hold it! I went right back down into the pit with this thing on top of my knees.

The supply man whose office was adjacent to the pits saw what happened and called the boss, who was very nasty about it. "Well, there's nothing wrong with him. Just fix him up with some Band-Aids." My knees were gashed and bleeding, so the supply man says, "No, no. You'd better send this man to the hospital." So now I'm back in General Hospital again. The doctor gave me pills once again for terrible pain, and I was sent home and off work for a while. Over the next month my knees would swell up but they never took any X-rays. I finally got back to work again in autumn of 1974, on light duty. I had to check buses. It involved lots of walking and getting on and off many times a day. So one day I slipped coming off. My knee gave way on me and I went down onto the pavement. This time the doctor not only X-rayed my knee, but shot dye into it and found that all this time I had been walking around on torn cartilage. He operated immediately.

I was beginning to think alcohol was my best friend. It seemed to be the only release I had and I was drinking every day. I was playing the game of Russian roulette. It was medication in the daytime and drinking at night. Then later on, I was drinking along with the medication as well. I had many accidents because I was drinking and driving my car. Most of the accidents were minor— sideswipes. things like that. I can remember the first major one I had: I ran through a stop sign, hit a guy dead center. Of course, the guy let me go because I told him I'd fix his car. He was a nice guy, and he agreed to it. So there were no police involved. I fixed his car and my own. My God was definitely looking out for me.

*T*he next major accident was with a brand new Chevy. I had given a kid a ride. I was on my way to the liquor store to get some booze. This kid needed a ride into the hills of Bernal Heights. After I let him out I got a little lost. I was driving up one of those steep hills out there and something happened to the car and I lost control. I started going down the hill, backwards, sideswiping about seven cars until I finally crashed into a fire hydrant, which ended up sitting where I was. It pushed my head into the steering wheel and drenched me with water. When I came to in the hospital, I found my shoes and walked out against the doctor's warnings, caught the bus, and went home. The next morning I was awful sore in the chest.

I turned to my savior, hard liquor—vodka, bourbon, scotch, gin. I was drinking around the clock at that time. The worst thing about the drinking was when I'd wake up in the morning and find I didn't have any liquor left. I was beginning to experience blackouts.

Anyway, after I wrecked that car, I bought another one. Two months later, I fell asleep at the wheel, ran up onto the sidewalk, and tore up everything from underneath the car. The place I bought it from offered me $20 for it. I could get four-fifths of vodka with $20. It sounded good to me!

What with the blackouts, I would tend to forget where I lived. Sometimes I'd park in someone else's garage, and sometimes I would forget completely where I parked the car. I remember this one incident: I parked the car, went into this place, drank, and shot pool. When I came out at closing time, I couldn't find the car. The next day the police found the car right in the center of town.

I still don't know how it got there.

Even the lowly companions I hung around with told me I was in the wrong business. I didn't fit in there. I never could. On the other hand, everything I had been taught as a kid was completely gone out the window. I started laughing at churchgoers, calling them rip-off artists. Deep down, I felt kind of bad about mocking them, but I would do it because of the booze. I'd be sitting there drinking gin from a big flower vase, laughing and joking about church and the "hypocrites" who went there.

At that time, boozing was much more of a priority than even women. I didn't want to be tied down and I knew that somehow, deep down, I couldn't hang onto a woman while drinking so much booze. So I developed the idea that maybe I'd never get married because marriage wasn't really for me, and the best thing for me to do was to just shack up for a while, and that was it.

*A*fter my compensation of $52.50 a week ran out, I lost my home. Saul, my fellow photographer, kept up the notes on the house for awhile, but then wanted his money. So I signed a release for him to sell the house. One day the bell rang. I went to the door pretty well soused out, and I saw this large truck back up. The driver said, "Do you live here?" I said, "Yes, this is my home." He said, "No, it's not any more, because I bought it." He put all my stuff in the huge garage, and moved his belongings into the house. During the night almost everything I owned disappeared from the garage except for a little refrigerator. This guy hadn't bothered to close the garage door, and I guess people just helped themselves. Saul ended up finding me a real small apartment and paid the rent for a couple of months, and then I got a break.

I was called back to Muni. They wanted me for a watchman-type position. It was light duty because I was still not in good shape. Meanwhile, I ended up in jail for carrying a weapon on the streets. It was an "in" thing to carry a gun in the pool rooms. Anyway, I lost my gun during a fight, and the cops found it. God was with me that night. Anything could have happened out there, being a black guy and in the wrong place. I could have gotten myself killed. I was shooting pool with a white guy. I caught a couple of guys cheating and this guy called me a name. So we headed outside and as I walked out the door, his buddy bopped me. I lost the fight to four men and the police. That was a close call.

I didn't drink until I got off from work, but I didn't realize that due to my daily habit, the booze was never really out of my system. On one occasion I went into the office of Comrade X, a great friend, and I had a seizure. The medics carted me off to the hospital. Strangely enough, they never identified it as an alcohol problem. A short time later, I was found in my apartment having another seizure by Comrade X's brother. I was totally out of my mind. They had to put me in a straitjacket. When I returned for my follow-up visit to the hospital doctor, this nurse came running down the hall after me. "Gee, you know it took four people to put you in a straitjacket! I thought we had lost you! I didn't think you were going to make it." She told me I was trying to set my hospital roommate's bed on fire with some matches I claimed were given me by somebody who instructed me to set his bed on fire. They had to put me in a room by myself. That was total insanity.

Around the same time, the cops found me drunk on the street, walking toward a liquor store. I had just parked my car after giving someone a lift. They took me to the jail and locked me up until 3:00 in the morning, when the jailer released me. So there I was, out on the streets, man, and at that time of the morning. I didn't know where my car was, and I wondered how I would get to it. I only had fifty cents. Having no idea where I was, I walked about two blocks and then saw garbagemen making their pickup. I saw this black guy so I told him I just got out of jail and was trying to find my car. From my description of where I parked it, he sent me walking in the right direction. I found it around daybreak. The toll to cross back to San Francisco over the bridge was fifty cents, which was exactly what I had. God continued to watch over me.

In the midst of all this chaos, there was something I got real early that allowed me to survive all this: some kind of sanity. Even then there was this glimmer of sanity that I got from the church, my mother, or my father early on. That's what those guys in the pool halls were seeing when they told me I was in the wrong business and didn't belong there. They saw something in me that they felt they could trust.

I actually felt protected by these guys. I ran into less racism, whether black or white, in those pool halls. They treated me with a certain dignity even when I was totally drunk and doing things I wouldn't do otherwise. I managed to hold on to some kind of integrity. Even in my madness, my background was still at my core.

*T*here was this fellow who owned a few things around the area, who had a few prostitutes and what-have-you. His main lady was his "wife." I felt she wanted to get away from him. She was a good person and he was pretty cold toward her. I just had a feeling that she wanted to escape. Now this guy was nice to me, very nice, and he trusted me but he was a crook. He was one of the guys who said, "You don't belong in this." So one day, after he beat her up pretty bad, she asked me to give her a ride to her mother's place. I had nerve enough to come by the house and pick her up. I didn't know what her reaction would be; I only knew that she was beat up, and she'd been told he wanted her to get out. So while I was loading some of her things into the car, he came by and told me I had broken the code. And bopped me right in the mouth. I didn't fight back because I wasn't armed at that particular time. That was one of the rare times that I didn't have the gun. I was sitting there trying to get my wits together when his wife comes running out of the house with her two kids and jumps into my car. He ran after her and jumped into the backseat, and I knew he had a gun. I turned around and put my hand under my jacket and told him, "I've known you for a long time, and you know me. Now you're in my car and I don't want you to do anything funny, but I want you to get out of my car right now." Strangely enough, as I was looking him right in the eyes, he just got out of the car. And I just drove right off with his lady. I don't know why he didn't shoot me. He could've shot me. I didn't have anything. I was bluffing, but it was just that type of look that I had in my eyes when I told him to get out of the car. He knew I wasn't kidding.

I used to take off and drive all over to get away at a moment's notice. I drove down to Los Angeles this one time and tried to persuade this lady I knew to go to Tijuana with me. She chickened out. I stopped off to visit a friend in Riverside and then took off for Mexico. I was by myself, drinking rum and coke. I had a fifth of rum in the car trunk. I put it in a coke bottle to drink while driving, and not be seen. When I got to San Diego, it suddenly dawned on me that I've got to have insurance and I can't speak Spanish. But I just kept going. It's a funny thing how, when you're drinking, you gravitate to drinking people. You know exactly where to go. I went into this service station and told them I was looking for somebody who spoke Spanish or who could tell me how to get some insurance when I got down to Tijuana. The service guy said, "Well, I think I know just the guy you want. His name is Joe. He goes to the horse races all the time and he's trying to get a ride down."

He gave me Joe's address and when I got there, some man told me, "Well, Joe's having lady problems, but he's gonna be here pretty soon." Finally he showed up and we made a deal, a ride for him to Tijuana in exchange for him helping me find some insurance. He jumped in the car and we had our drinks and shot down to Tijuana. It was a hard job trying to buy insurance in Tijuana without getting ripped off, but Joe finally got me to some bank and they sold me the insurance. Then I took him to the racetrack and then went back into the city. The place was full of prostitutes. Even then, something in me wanted to go somewhere more decent.

*S*o I decided to go down to Ensenada. The highways down to Ensenada were so bad, they were like pure rock—better for wagons than cars. I met this white dude from El Paso down there who was chasing some strip dancer he actually wanted to marry. This cat matched my drinking and he had money, man! He just floated us with booze. I'd listen to his crying and we'd talk and strategize while drinking, about how he was gonna have a good time with this chick. We cried in our soup together and finally I got tired, because I was paralyzed without any money. So I split and came on back home to San Francisco. All the way home I kept refilling my coke bottle from the fifth of rum in the trunk. And I got waved right over the border!

Once the sixty-six weeks of compensation ended, I was hustling for jobs, but no one would hire me because of my physical problems. I really didn't know what to do. I checked with the general assistance people and they told me they could give me $50 worth of food stamps for $30! Things were going bad and I drove my poor sister crazy. She was the only one close by and she told me she was sick and tired of the mess. Saul, Comrade X, my closest friend, helped me keep the apartment on Hayes Street.

Then they called me back to work and asked me what I could do. I said, "You'll have to tell me." I ended up as a guard. But of course, the other guys who worked as guards didn't like the idea of a bus driver coming in on this "clique" kind of job, so I had a few opponents there. Yet somehow, the ball stuck with me and the personnel person who got me the job stuck with me, too. It seemed to work out. I was both drinking and pilling then, and I always kept a small bottle in my locker. I got too drunk. I had a whole pile of punched "in and out" time cards I had swiped, and I'd just put my name and date on the card so I would get paid anyway. This time card scam let me sneak out and drink and not get docked. The boss knew I was on heavy medication for pain so he probably dismissed what might have otherwise appeared suspicious in my mannerisms. As for the rest of the guys, a lot of them were drinking too, but they were not in the shape I was in.

Then a strange thing began to happen. I kept running into this guy at work. I'd be going down the stairs and he'd be coming up the stairs. He would ask me if I needed some help and if I wanted to talk to him. I halfway knew what he wanted, but I didn't want anything to do with him. I tried to avoid him and then one day there he was again, saying, "If you wanna talk, we'll talk." And he just kept on walking. Then something just struck me—what was with this guy? So I said, "Wait a minute! What do you want to talk to me about?" He took me into an office, sat me down, and told me about the AA fellowship program he belonged to. He asked me if I wanted to go. I said yes.

PART V

Coming Out: Spiritual Awakening

*I*t was something about Ben's story and also the questions that he asked me, like when and how I drank and how I was causing myself and everybody else problems. Finally he asked me, "Do you want to do something about all this?" That's when I agreed to attend the fellowship the next day. Meanwhile, I was too soused to walk home, so he asked his friend to give me a ride home all the way over to Hayes Street. I had my head back on the seat, "drunk resting," and as we were coming over Highway 280 merging to 101, something just sort of ran through me. I opened my eyes and looked up at the sky. I saw a pretty light in the whole sky, which I've only seen that one time—some colors of the rainbow, but not a rainbow. The beautiful light was touching me as it transformed the sky. My life changed from that moment on. I had a feeling of being rejuvenated in my mind (not my body, which was weak). It cleared my mind—boom! Like that! That must've been my spiritual awakening, because it was one of the most unbelievable sights that I had ever seen!

I was looking right through the windshield when I saw this sight, but I couldn't respond because I was too zapped out with the alcohol in my system. I asked the driver what happened and he said, "Nothing." When we got to my apartment, he practically had to carry me up the stairs. He put me in the bed and I stayed there all night thinking about what I had seen. It went on right through the night. And sure enough, that guy Ben came by and picked me up to take me to the fellowship the next morning.

That day I asked the landlady to throw all my liquor out. I told her I didn't want it. At this point, I had lost my home, my business, and wrecked my cars, and I had the least skilled job I ever had before in my life. I had no savings and hadn't paid any of my credit cards, not to mention any other bills. I also had no companion, no relationship with a woman. By the time Ben got to me, I knew there was something wrong, that I needed a solution. I needed somebody to tell me what to do. Ben was the first person who said, "I can get you some help. I know some folks who can help you." That had never been conveyed to me before or I was not ready to accept help or advice before that time.

At first I was unable to connect this illuminating experience I had in the car with God. I had stayed away from church for such a long time. I couldn't quite connect the meaning of this experience or anything about what was happening. It was a little frightening. I guess I just simply had too much alcohol in my system. I knew something great and grand had happened, but I didn't know what it was! However, I did tell Ben about it, and that was when he talked about a Higher Power, a spiritual awakening.

A few weeks later he called me on a Sunday morning and asked if I would like to go to church with him. Immediately I was frightened, because I thought I didn't belong in church because of my past. The worst thought was imagining how people would look at me! Here I am still shaking and all this, and so I said, "Er, no, I don't think so. I've got a meeting to go to at 3:00." Ben said, "Fine. Church starts at 11:00, and that will give you plenty of time to get out and go to a meeting."

I didn't really protest too much, so Ben picked me up and took me to a Presbyterian church, introduced me to the pastor—Dr. Hannibal Williams—and to a small group of people. I was shocked to have the pastor share some of his story with me, and he had had the same experience with alcohol. I couldn't believe this! These two people, Ben and the pastor, looking this good and they had gone through the same thing I was going through! I was really impressed. I became even more eager to go to the meetings and hear everyone's stories.

Once I stopped drinking, a lot of things happened and I started to see a lot more as well. I went through a lot of problems. I was shaking constantly, feeling very nervous, and had several seizures. I couldn't eat. Nothing would stay down. I couldn't sleep. I had terrible nightmares. Ben got me through the detox period step by step. He told me what to do and I followed it to the letter. I kept thinking, "What the heck? If he can do this thing, then I can do it, too."

Until I met Ben, I didn't know what to do, even though I knew something was wrong. I simply was at the point of no return; I just didn't think anything could be done anyway. When Ben told me his story and I was looking at him and seeing how clean he was, I couldn't believe it. You mean I can get back to looking like this? His bottom was even worse than mine and he came back, so why couldn't I come back from all this? That was the hope his story gave me. And not only was his story hope-filled, but he was a living sign of hope, when he kept his word the next day and came to take me to the program, even though he himself had to go to work. He parked right out front and told me, "Go to the door. They'll take care of you."

*W*hen I walked through that door, surprisingly, I was the only black guy there! There was a whole building full of white people and they were welcoming me. And not only were they welcoming me, but they had gotten out of this mess I was in! My first question was to ask them what to do about the shakes. One guy told me, "When you sit down, sit on your hands." And that's what I did. I sat on my hands to keep them from shaking. There was this one little lady, she was very nice. She just talked to me and held my hands, and then she said, "That's all right. Just keep on with it until it stops." Then she asked me if I wanted some coffee. I got the cup about halfway up to my face, and whoosh! It just went into my face and nose. I was trying to grasp and hold the coffee cup in my shaking hand, but I couldn't.

I constantly talked to Ben at work. When I'd get the shakes I would go down the street and use the pay phone to call him. He was good about listening and making suggestions. And I needed that closeness because I hadn't had that except for my sister, who was really waiting for me to hit bottom. Ben suggested that I get myself a Bible to keep my mind busy. So I read it at lunchtime, break time, and in between. The rest of my free time I walked, up and down and all around. Ben also gave me the Big Book from the AA Program. I didn't understand a lot of things either from the Bible or the Big Book, but Ben told me to just go ahead and read through it. "You can always ask someone if there's something you don't understand, as long as you're going someplace where they're explaining. Then it will be revealed to you." And a lot of what I read that I did not understand was eventually revealed to me. I would hear it at church and say, "Oh—that's what that meant." So if you can bring the body there and sit there and listen, it will be revealed to you what you read; you don't have to understand it.

In that same space of time, my private doctor set me up for a psychiatric appointment. Some of the city doctors were saying I was crazy and that I didn't have any sense, or that I was goofing off. So he set me up for the appointment but it was a long wait— a couple of months down the line before it would be my turn. Finally after I was sober, I had the appointment and the first thing the psychiatrist asked me was, "Do you think you might have a problem? You know, I think you might have a problem." And I said, "Yes." Then he said, "What are you doing about it?" After I explained how I was in the program he just stood up and said, "If you know what it is and you're doing something about it, there's no use in talking."

I liked that. He didn't give me any pills and I didn't want any. The pills stopped when the drinking stopped. That was very dangerous. I had been seeing different doctors for different things and they were all giving me pills—Darvon, Stelazine, Librium—but it all stopped at the same time. I wouldn't wish anyone to go through that experience. It was very dangerous. Ben and the fellowship people were there for me through all of that withdrawal. There were times when I would crave a drink and I'd run down to the corner phone and call someone and say, "I feel like I want a drink. What can I do?" They'd tell me to have some ice cream or a candy bar and remind me to come to the Bible study at Howard Presbyterian Church, that they'd be looking for me there. That's exactly what I needed: somebody to tell me what to do. The doctors obviously didn't know anything to tell me. They just wrote me off as crazy or something. Also, there was the small group of folks at the church who seemed to take to me very well, and I would be very honest with them, admitting I had a problem. They never seemed disturbed, but just accepted me for where I was. There was this one lady, a very strong lady who took care of the little kids. She would invite me to sit with her at the park while she watched them play. Somehow, sitting and talking with her helped me catch on to what the church was all about, and I officially joined. Dr. Hannibal Williams, the pastor, celebrated by taking Ben and me out to a restaurant, and I had the first meal that I really enjoyed—ham and eggs. Boy! That was uplifting, to be able to get down a meal. That was about two to three weeks after I stopped drinking. By a year later, I was Sunday school teacher for those kids I had watched in the park.

PART VI

Giving Something Back:
The Liberation House Story

In 1974, shortly after I stopped drinking, I reinjured myself, collapsing on my knees again as I stepped off the bus on the wrong foot. After a sonogram, the doctor ordered immediate surgery. When I awoke from surgery Dr. Williams was the person sitting at my bedside. He prayed for me and urged me to call him if I needed help. A week later, I was back in my apartment, unable to care for myself, with my whole leg bandaged up. I was laying there worrying about who was going to help me, when my landlady, who I had never met before, arrived out of nowhere. She told me she never does this kind of thing, but God was telling her to take care of me. That was definitely my Higher Power at work for me! She and I got to be very good friends. I would say to her, "You know, I can't pay you. I don't know when I can pay you." She would always answer, "Well, I'm praying for you and don't worry about the money. I'm just gonna do what a Christian's supposed to do." She eventually retired to San Antonio and I visited her each time I went to Texas to see my mother. Later on, through my doctor's efforts, the city decided to send me $300 to cover the cost of someone caring for me during that time. I told her about it and she told me to keep $75 of it for myself. I visited her until she passed away.

Through my landlady, Ben, and many others like them, my Higher Power became more and more real to me. I started remembering childhood stories I had heard about Jesus from the Bible, and it all started to click. I began to develop a close personal relationship with Christ, clearly seeing Him as my Savior. It made more sense to me than anything else. In understanding Christ's love for me, the experience on the freeway seems definitely to have been a spiritual awakening—or should I say, a reawakening of all I had been exposed to as a child. Prayer was a part of every breathing moment of my mother's life, and now I do a lot of praying.

A big part of my spiritual renewal was being accepted by all the people at Howard Presbyterian Church. When my drinking became a disease, I felt like I was not worthy and that nobody would want to bother with me any more. It was amazing to me that the church would take that much time with me! I needed to tell them again and again that I was a recovering person. Every time the pastor would give me a task, like Sunday school teaching, I kept thinking maybe they forgot where I had come from. Eventually, I was ordained a deacon and then an elder, one of the ruling elders of the church. I had nothing to do with it. They saw something in me and responded from their hearts. All the acceptance, caring, and love that I experienced from these people and those in the program inspired me to believe in what I was reading about Christ's message. All the things He was talking about while He was here were happening for me right then in my life. People were reaching out and helping in all the ways that they could help. The little things they asked me to do at church gave me great encouragement, gave me a lot of confidence. And then the pastor accomplishing so many great works after having been down the same road as me—this was a great inspiration to me. And the Bible fit right in with the program, which gave me tools for dealing with resentments and other things that might affect me and make me want to drink.

When I think back to when I started drinking at fifteen, I don't know if I would have started drinking had I been with friends who didn't drink. I had no idea that drugs and alcohol sooner or later catch up and rob you . . . sort of like borrowing from the future only to find no future when you get there. That's what drugs and alcohol will do for you.

I worked the program wholeheartedly because I was totally at rock bottom. I had nothing, no one at all, so it was like starting all over again, like a little child. I was told things to do and they made sense to me. If you said, "Walk," I walked. I didn't run. So it was just that simple, step-by-step thing. And then of course in the background and kind of overhead, pulling all this together for me, was this thing that happened to me on the freeway. The feeling that I had that everything was gonna be okay; it's gonna be all right; don't worry.

AA members, Ben who was black and Joy (the one who held my hand), a white woman, and their stories were equally powerful for me. All through my life I had met good whites and good blacks, bad whites and bad blacks. I was open to Joy's support as well as to Ben's help and care. When I first heard Ben's story, my reaction was, Boom! "My God, I wasn't that bad, but if he can do this, I can do this, too." Then I heard Joy's story and it was twice as bad as Ben's, yet she overcame this thing. And I thought, "My God! They went through all this? Well, if they can do it, I can do it." Remember, all my life I had that attitude that if somebody could do something, I could figure out a way I could do it as well. That's how I looked at sobriety. There's a whole lot of ways to do it and whatever way fits you best, then you have to pursue that road. I could not be a copy of Ben or of Joy. I had to learn how to live with me and figure out some kind of way that I was gonna make it through this thing. Because if I didn't do this thing, I was gonna die, man, surely! I was on my way to the graveyard, no doubt about it. That moment on the freeway, it was 1:00 AM, and in the night sky I saw light. Wow! April 24, 1973.

Something shifted me back to that other strain of myself, that was nurtured by my family. It was some time during the mid-1970's that the "hustler" part of me, so evident in the pool halls, etc., started working for the Lord. I started to get involved with

Liberation House, which had been Dr. Hannibal Williams' dream. I would attend the board meetings and sit there and listen to these high-positioned people, but I would not talk, just listen, because I felt they were a lot more educated than I was. I was nominated as third vice chair, but I never really had anything to do. Dr. Hannibal Williams had gathered these people together on the board in 1973, but by 1975, they began falling away because of conflicts of interest and other various reasons. The chairman himself had to resign because he was getting a promotion and could no longer give it the time. Everyone else was equally busy, so all at once, they looked to me. "You're going to have to take this over as chairman." Now I was very touched by Dr. Williams' vision for Liberation House, and I wanted to be involved in it all the way, but I didn't know if I could handle being chairman. Dr. Williams promised he would help me, so even though I knew nothing about counseling and even less about chairmanship, there was nobody else to do it there. I was in the midst of this black community, being asked to take charge by a man who had groomed me exclusively for the task!

When I took over as chairman we were still trying to get organized. We had an outreach office but no real place, just sort of revolving around meetings at the church and different places like that. Meanwhile, Dr. Williams was trying to raise funds for the program. In order to get money from the city you had to go through what's called proposal writing. We applied for a grant and the city said (would you believe?), "We didn't know black people had drinking problems. You need to do a survey to prove to us that there are enough black people for us to warrant you a contract with some monies to take care of this." At this time Dr. Williams, who was vice chair of the citywide alcoholism committee, sought and received $15,000 to do a survey of the black community. We hired a director whose name has slipped my mind to do the work.

So we had to get out and walk the pavement with our survey forms. I spent days with that thing. After I turned it in, the city decided that it didn't answer the question after all. Then they told us to do another proposal just devoted to asking for funding of $45,000.

Meanwhile, we opened our first office on Divisadero Street. I had the job of driving people for help. This was my first car since I had gotten sober, a '63 Comet for $350 which made a whole lot of noise. My phone was open to callers in trouble throughout the night. Everyone seemed to call between 3:00 and 4:00 in the morning. I'd have to go get them and bring them to the detox at Osnan Center. This was the only place to bring blacks because they couldn't get into the better programs. That's the main reason why Dr. Williams had founded Liberation House.

I knew nothing about real estate or politics, but we set out to find a house. Dr. Williams was able to obtain a house from the S.F. Redevelopment Agency that had been acquired by the city through eminent domain. He paid $1,100 out of his own pocket and made a successful bid to rehabilitate the property. The house was a handyman's special and it was just down the street from the office. It would be a temporary dwelling until we could find a better house. In the meantime, we submitted a proposal to the city for $45,000. Finally, on a Tuesday evening in 1976 they called me to a meeting to talk about the proposal. "We're going to let you have the $45,000 under certain conditions. You will have to work from a line-item budget." They had broken it down and worked it all out as to what I could spend for linens, what I could spend for janitorial supplies, office supplies, cooking utensils, etc. They told me to go to whatever stores I chose, have them write up my order, price it within this line-item limit, and get it all back to them by 4:00 PM on Friday. I had to buy $45,000 worth of items in three days! So I now said a prayer, "God, if this is Your will, okay."

I went out and got in the car and first thing that jumped into my mind was "I've got to talk to Dr. Williams about this business right now." He was in the process of founding a new church, and was real busy. When I gave him the news he said, "Well, you know you can do it, but you need some help." Two board members agreed to help get the prices on the linens and the kitchen utensils. I focused on getting the costs for office and janitorial supplies. As I made phone calls trying to get prices many of the people just hung up on me. Finally, I found a supply house whose manager referred me to his best salesperson, and she assisted me the entire day. I mean, we didn't take one break. She was sold on the idea and she really worked with me! We had to keep crunching the numbers to keep within the budget, and that was tricky. But by the grace of God, I had the budget on the city's desk by 4:00 PM Friday. I said, "Well, here it is! It's all here on paper here. The merchandise is ready to go." So they really had no choice but to go ahead and give it to me. And that was how in 1976 I signed the first contract from the city for Liberation House.

We took the name Liberation House from Dr. Williams, who had founded the New Liberation Presbyterian Church in 1973.

The next step was to find two people with sobriety in order to meet the requirements for a live-in facility. Another program sent two black guys over and I talked to them and counseled them and told them what was happening. So with the permission of their directors, they left their program and joined Liberation House as my first two sober residents. They had been in recovery for about four months. The facility itself was a small Victorian, two-story apartment building. We had a couple of rooms downstairs and about three rooms upstairs. Our office was still down the street. We had to buy some secondhand furniture which we paid for ourselves, since it wasn't on the city's list.

The other requirement was that I attend some counseling training along with my supervision from Dr. Williams. I was able to meet that requirement because I had already attended a one-semester course at State University and received a certificate. So I made it through on that one for the time being. By now I had been sober about three years. Around this time, much to my distress, I was called by the National Council on Alcoholism to do a talk for a drunk driving class. So I conferred with Dr. Williams and we came to the conclusion that it might be helpful to these people as well as myself. I was relieved to hear that it was only a small group. But when I got up there I was totally shocked! There were about 250 people waiting to hear what I had to say. I did do the pitch but I was pretty shaky and after I finished I left immediately. Prayer got me through that one.

Then they called me back again and I said, "Well, okay. Just this one time. But you fooled me the other time. You had a whole house full." To which they replied, "Well, we promise this time there won't be that many." Well, it was that many! Then I got a third call and I tried to explain how busy I was with Liberation House and my job as well.

Finally I agreed to do it one last time. To which they replied, "When you come up this time, we might have a surprise for you." So I went up and did my pitch and after it was over they invited me out to dinner. Unknowingly, I had just spoken to professionals, with degrees and everything else. The boss was there as well and we talked and talked at dinner when she suddenly said, "You know, how would you like to become one of our staff?" I said, "Staff? This is really heavy stuff, here, now! I don't have the experience and I don't have the education." They reassured me that they would teach me what I needed to know. I told them I had to think about all this and I thought about it long and hard for a good week. Then Dr. Williams and I discussed it at length. So, I decided to give it a try. My instruction began and Dr. Williams was a constant counselor, always there to support and advise, and to fight the good fight! When it came to the folks downtown, you could always call on Dr. Hannibal Williams to stand up to them and to stand up for you!

I only had to be there once a week for three hours on Thursday evening. They held the classes at the old Fireman's Fund building on California Street. I learned how to facilitate a group of from twelve to fifteen people. Shortly after I began this training, they decided that I didn't need any more because I already knew what I was doing, and so I began my formal job of facilitating for them for the next four years, about one day or night a week.

*T*hese groups got me in touch with different people who took an interest in Liberation House, and that made my task easier. People were coming on board with different ideas and I had to get into this thing of hiring and firing. When on more than one occasion it was necessary to fire a self-seeking counselor or director, Dr. Williams was solidly there to back me up. Some disgruntled employees even attempted lawsuits, but we stood fast.

All the while I was still doing the info clerk job full-time at Muni. I was also doing a lot of volunteering at church, working with the poor, visiting the sick. All this involvement helped to overcome the constant pain I was in every day. The back thing and the leg thing hadn't gone anyplace. I wasn't taking any of the old pain pills at that time so whenever I had withdrawal flareups, I called Dr. Williams or Ben. I was able to handle it and not go back to anything addictive.

I had a very occasional social life. I could take a lady out to dinner or something, but real close stuff, no. That was my life then, caring and trying to help people help themselves. And I was helping myself at the same time. There just wasn't any room for close relationships during that time span.

I really started a whole new life. I was told by people who had successfully stayed sober to live everything totally differently from how I had been living it when I was drinking. When I went out with friends, I even ate fried chicken instead of a steak, because steak and wine went together in my past.

One major part of my past became much more clarified for me once I got sober, and that was the racism I had encountered all along the way. I was much more aware of it, more sensitive to it—but more able to handle it without getting upset to the point where it hurt me. I know exactly what is happening now at all times. Before, I just got real angry and wasn't quite sure what was happening. I just wanted to fight then, whereas now I can handle it in a different way. I always believed from my childhood that there are good folks in all races. I remember an incident when I first went up to Muni to be an information clerk. They put me with this black guy to train me. This was shades of the wallpaper company back in Houston. This guy seemed to just hate my guts. He didn't want anything to do with me. If I was slow reading the map, he'd just have a fit. Meanwhile, another boss was watching all this and he came over one day and asked me if I would prefer working with someone else. "I sure would," was my immediate response. And so this white guy became my trainer and we hit it off, just like that. His positive attitude freed me up and I learned all about that job in my old, tried-and-true way. I memorized all the information in those books—the streets, the bus schedules, etc. I ended up becoming the trainer. As a clerk, I trained the guys who became bosses over me. Frankly, I had no desire to put in for a higher position; my desire then was to help other people help themselves, in order to help myself have a sober life.

As I was saying, once I got sober, I was more aware of racism, the quiet racism that is a hidden part of everyday life. I take you out to a restaurant, you're white and I'm black. I'm treating you to dinner, but when the waitress brings the bill, she places it in front of you. I tell her I'm taking care of it and go into my pocket and give her the cash. She brings back the change and hands it to you. Another time, I'm standing talking with a white guy and somebody comes up, stands next to me, and looks right through me and asks the white guy some questions about directions or something, and there I am looking right at the guy. Being sober helps me laugh at things like that now. It's the other person's problem, not mine. I try not to take it to heart.

Getting sober can be a relearning of life; it can bring you to a whole different level. For the first two years in the program, I dealt with whites far more than blacks, and it brought me to understand them better, and to feel better understood by them as well. The program touches every part of your life if you're working it, and frees you up to make choices. When I'm sober and clearheaded, I have a choice not to react to the sickness that I'm seeing and meeting in those streets. When I read racism in someone's eyes, white or black, I can make a choice to deal with it without anger. It's called surrender. The fellow in the marine corps with me finally just surrendered when he said, "Hey, I made a mistake here." It was a self confession, the best thing in the world. And I'm certain he felt much better about the whole thing because he cleared his conscience. I don't know whether or not he got killed in Korea, or what happened, but he got that off of himself.

Boozing and drugging steals away all intelligent thinking. It's called "stinking thinking." Alcohol and dope do not let you think rationally. Once you become sober and away from it, you can use those "corrupt" thinking experiences to your advantage. That's what it's all about. You don't live in the past; you learn from it.

*B*y 1977 I was ready to meet Florence. She was a member of New Liberation Church and we would meet at Sunday School classes and Bible studies. Then she became a board member of Liberation House, but we didn't start dating until the latter part of 1978. I was sober about five years at the time. It was around the same time that we got our first house, temporary, with five beds. It was hard for Florence and me to find time together because whenever I had spare time, I would be at Liberation House or on the phone, counseling. I was also speaking around the city. Any time anyone called me and asked me to tell my story, I agreed, and Florence would often go with me. She was well aware of all that was happening. She knew exactly what I was into. We talked about our decision to get married for quite some time and sought the counsel of the pastor, who approved and gave us his blessing. Again, there were choices to make. Florence had three kids of her own, and I had to turn loose some of the things that I was involved with, such as a chairmanship with the Cancer Society. I was always moving out into some other area. My Higher Power always seemed to have me getting something started or moving to some other place. Some slot would open and God would fit me into it. Of course, Liberation House was my continual commitment. Florence and I married in 1979. Her youngest child was nine at the time.

I was deep into Muni. My job as information clerk there was a tough one. I was real good at it. I would answer the question before they finished asking me. But still it wasn't that simple. People would start telling me their problems; sometimes they'd curse and call me all kinds of names. You got to listen to a lot of different things. Actually, I was the first person with whom bus riders would come in contact, and I'd hear it all. It was an experience and I learned a lot. Eventually, I was even awarded for my service. That gave me a lot of incentive. I was getting off the elevator one day and one of the managers stopped me in the hall to tell me how much I had changed. It really lifts you up to hear somebody say their idea of you was wrong! All these little goodies kept me moving and got me through the screaming and cursing part of the job.

In 1990 I got the Gold Award for outstanding performance contributing to the service, quality, and efficiency of the Muni Railway. Later, I began to receive lots of certificates from different people. I got one from Senator Marks, one from the California legislature, a certificate of recognition from Assemblyman John Burton, and a certificate of honor from the Board of Supervisors, City of San Francisco. I received an honor award for outstanding service from the Service Employees International Union, AFL/CIO, and a Distinguished Employee Certificate of Merit from the mayor's office, along with other system-wide certificates of recognition. The Muni Railway gave me $100 and a gift certificate for Florence and me to a fancy restaurant downtown.

*U*ntil my sobriety, racism played a big role in the direction my life was going. I was always limited to some area that was a dead-end street. I was never given that extra shot. It was like when the photography instructor kept insisting that I go farther with my talents and I never had the money to buy the supplies that would help me to do that. So I never really had the backing that I needed to excel in anything. Then I got sober and saw I could excel within the scope of what I made up my mind to do, and that was to help myself by helping other people to help themselves.

My mother always taught me that I had to work to survive and be a man in this world, and in order to achieve anything. There has always been a lot of work in my life. When I had this job with Muni, I was cofounding Liberation House, and in reality I was acting as director, chairman, counselor—the whole bit—for nine years, along with my chairmanship with the Cancer Society. The Spirit of God was always moving inside of me to change the outside of me. My listening to that inner thing, and acting on it, brought about the steady change in my life. And that movement, that change, is all about service, helping people. That's who I am! I have reached that conclusion with my God, and that is my goal for the rest of my life!

My son was born when I was fifty years old, and my daughter when I was fifty-five. As a father, I can see a lot of advantages my past life brings to my parenthood. When we see some guy on drugs or drunk on the street, I tell my kids this is what happens and I remind them that they don't see the people this disease kills. I do my best to be a good model to my kids. Sometimes, you don't really know when you are doing your best, or how much you have to do to do this, but I'm just trying to shape my kids' minds into knowing that there's someone else beyond me who also loves them. There is something much greater than I am, and that is God, their loving Father in Heaven. My wife and I try to give our kids the teachings of Christ in our everyday life.

I started work when I was fifteen years old. I didn't really have time to play like the other kids. I really missed the adolescent stage. That's what's so great about being the father of a very active sports lover. My son goes right from one season to the next and we go right on around through basketball, soccer, and baseball. Being with him in that space gives me a lot of what I missed. I remember a guy I was working with, and he was at his desk and I was at my desk, and all of a sudden, I'd feel like rolling up a ball of paper and popping him on the head. And he'd do likewise to me. So it's sort of like acting out the adolescent stage that I missed. Not only did I have to become Mr. Responsibility when my dad left, but drinking cut short my adolescence as well. Sometimes, alcohol keeps you adolescent and sometimes it cuts it short.

The Long Cane Creek Bridge reveals one of the themes of my life. A kid in elementary school, I was assigned to go downtown and pick up the mail. It was a great responsibility. I had to cross the bridge and there was a nest of snakes on the far side that I had to pass. It was a very frightening thing for me but I was determined to act like a man and try doing it, even if I had to scoot and run once I passed those vipers. I did it, and I didn't complain. I didn't go back to the school whimpering and crying to the teacher that I was afraid of the snakes. No matter what, I was going to take care of business!

As an older parent, I found that my children help me be in the moment, that kind of one-day-at-a-time stuff. When my son was about a year old, I took him to the zoo, and he had a chance to touch things that I had never touched, and that was a good feeling.

After being sober more than twenty-seven years, I can tell you that when I cease to fear that I might drink again, then I don't have much time in these parts. The specific fear is a fear of losing the balance in my life. This is the whole thing that I'd like to carry over to my kids: that a lot of these things are part of human nature, but if we don't keep some balance, I think we're in trouble. Balance is the only way to survive racism. You say to yourself, "I am taking care of myself; I'm not going to be drawn into this sickness." I can understand that sickness better now than I could then. I can react to it differently now. I see the person with the racist attitude as having the problem. Whatever his problem is with me because of the color of my skin, then that is his problem, and I refuse to let him draw me into his sickness. I just don't choose to be sick any longer. Because I feel that a person who goes around hating folks puts himself in the most useless, wasteful, pitiful situation that a person can get himself into, and I don't care to even deal with that kind of person. I don't want to hang out with those people, doing that hating.

*I*n order to request some aid for Liberation House, it was recommended that I go to a man who supported nonprofit organizations. As soon as he opened his office door, I could see it in his eyes. He sat down and said, "Brad sent you over to me to ask for help, huh?" And I said, "Yes." And he said, "Well, I don't know why he wanted to do a thing like that, because he knows I don't support black programs." That was a bombshell to me and I had to sit there for just a second to get my composure together. Then I politely got up and thanked him, told him I was sorry I had wasted his time.

A year or so later, they gave a black person in the city a dinner downtown, and I was down there and this same man was there also. I walked right up to him, all dressed up in his tuxedo suit, and asked him how he was doing. He said, "I don't remember who you are." Then I told him, "You should remember me very well because I was in your office and you turned me down. Remember Liberation House?" He stood there like stone and I said, "You think about it, Sir, and you'll remember sooner or later." Then I left. He never looked at me any more that night. My whole experience with that guy was about dignity. Initially at the man's office, I thanked him and walked away. It reflected very well on Liberation House and on myself. Then later, I stood up for myself again and let him know that I was standing up for my race. I didn't let it pass. I believe this dignity came from the direction I had chosen for my life—the teachings of Christ, the most valuable, sensible, and simple way for me to go. It gives me peace of mind to know that you reap what you sow. When I drank, I sowed trouble and reaped poison. Now I am reaping dignity and peace.

My God and the resourcefulness and perseverance that have enabled me to keep Liberation House going actually came out of my drunkenness and messed up life. My past history gives me the energy, the excessive energy to keep carrying on. An alcoholic has boundless energy and perseverance. He'll even move mountains that stand between him and a drink. We just apply these same aspects to sober living. As you look back at how sick you were then you think of some other guy who is as sick now. If there's a way to help another guy, then why shouldn't you do it, knowing that you've also gone through it, alone? There's no longer any reason for someone to be shaking and trembling, trying to get to a phone before a seizure hits. The God that I believe in asks those of us who have gone through these things to heal the same brokenness in others and be there for them through all the challenges of recovery. Once you're in the hands of the Living God, you never know where He might put you—kind of like the prophets of the Bible.

*L*iberation House was the brainchild of Dr. Hannibal Williams. It was kind of a prophetic ministry because at that time, there was no place for blacks to recover and rehabilitate. Liberation House was founded for blacks specifically, but nobody of any color is ever excluded who has a problem. If that man who said to me, "I don't help black folks" hadn't prejudged, he would have found out that half the residents in the house were white. That has been my focal point all along, to help anyone who comes to us. Over 10,000 men have gone through our program, and half of them were white. Sometimes we have more whites than we have blacks. I think that's what impresses people when they come into Liberation House.

It's been a long fight to keep Liberation House open. Prayer has been the most powerful part of that struggle. I'm a strong believer in prayer, and I've had lots of people praying for me in this situation. I think that those prayers were answered through me in the success of Liberation House. There were a lot of people pulling for me then and now. They rallied behind me, and I still can go to them for some old-time advice, to just sit and talk. They seemed to know more about what direction I was going in than I did myself. Knowing that they were there praying for me gave me the motivation to keep on going. I draw on the strength of the black community, the prayer and connectedness, to keep on going. Dr. Williams, the man who founded this program, had a dream, and I latched onto that dream. And I wasn't going to give it up. I was going to stay with it until it floated or sank.

I believe that I have truly been blessed, that I am a walking miracle. It's a miracle from God that I'm here. It's a miracle that I could have a beautiful family. It's a miracle that I'm still taking one day at a time. It's a miracle that I don't want to forget about my past; I want to keep learning from it.

I carry myself in a way that keeps me far removed from the temptations of my past. Had I not gone through what I went through, I don't think I could be any more content or happier than I am now with my life. I don't have any idea what's in store for me later down the line. I'm just willing to give as much back as I possibly can and return what people have given me.

It's getting close to time for me to move on; time for someone younger to come up with other ideas and meet the challenges in a new way. And I'll just move along. I don't worry about what I'm going to do or what's going to come up next. I'm just waiting till it gets here and then we'll see what happens and what proceeds from there.

I have the greatest high of all—peace of mind! And that feels very free.

Letter of Thanks

I would like to say first that Curtis Jones has been a longtime confidant and friend. He has been with me on this road of recovery for close to eighteen years. I met Curtis at Liberation House in 1981. It was some time after being in counseling with him that I realized he was the cofounder and board chairman of Liberation House. I was struck by his humility. There was a quiet strength that I wanted. Later on I found out that Curtis, like myself, was a recovering person.

I am coming forward to acknowledge his life's work. I have been touched by his example in my own personal recovery. Curtis' writings will move and inspire the reader. Anyone in reading Curtis' personal experiences will be challenged to look within and see the common thread in all of us.

It is apparent his ministry in life has been one of being of service to others. Thousands of men who have come to Liberation House have been touched by this man. They have come like myself, alcoholic and substance-dependent, in search of a way out. He's been a true citizen to his community. Liberation House has become an institution in the Western Addition of San Francisco. The house has always reflected the diversity in that community and has given its residents tools for a new life.

In 1981, when I arrived at Liberation House, I was homeless. I was helpless, and hopelessly addicted to drugs and alcohol. I had a 10th-grade education, no work skills, and was a three-time loser in the penal system. During the nine months I was at Liberation House, I was able to stay clean and sober, complete my high school education, and become employable.

It is now seventeen plus years later, and I live in my own home. I have a college education. I have the love and respect of my family, children, and community. And my most precious and honored gift is my clean and sober life. My recovery is in direct relation to the people who have come before me, like Curtis—whose lives have changed regardless of all the odds to the contrary. My professional life continues to be rewarding. I'm a registered nurse. My opportunities are boundless. Curtis, throughout all of these years, has lived up to what he says: "Do what you say you're going to do"; "Be where you say you're going to be when you say you're going to be there"; Do the right thing for the right reasons"; and "Always look to God and not yourself for your strength and hope." I have learned I never have to walk alone or live that way ever again. "A day at a time."

Thanks a lot, Curtis!!

Michael D.

POSTSCRIPT

A BOSTON REPORT APPEARING IN THE
SAN FRANCISCO CHRONICLE
9/18/98:

"Whites Still Privileged, Race Panel Tells Clinton"

Thirty years ago, President Lyndon Johnson's Kerner
Commission concluded that America was moving toward two
societies, one black and one white, separate but unequal. Today,
after 15 months of study and hundreds of racial dialogues around
the country, President Clinton's Race Advisory Board describes a
somewhat different America—more united than divided along
racial lines, but a nation where discrimination is still a fact of life.

White privilege, the authors said, is built into the daily indig-
nities that minorities endure and whites generally do not. Whites
aren't followed by store detectives who see the word "shoplifter"
in the color of their skin. Board members said they had given an
apology for slavery considerable thought over the course of the
year. "We concluded the question of an apology for slavery itself is
much too narrow, in the light of the experience of blacks over the
course of this nation's history," they said. "The apology we must
all make cannot be adequately expressed in words, but in action."

Recently, I was in the downtown area of San Francisco on my way to a doctor's appointment. As I was early, I decided to stop into a well-known bookstore located in the area. Now, this is a very busy store, and at that particular time I'd say there were about ninety-nine percent white customers in the store. In fact, I didn't see any other blacks in the store. After spending some time looking around, although I didn't touch any of the books or periodicals, I decided to depart for my doctor's appointment. As I walked out of the front door surrounded by whites, the shoplifter alarm sounded, and within seconds this young white man wearing faded jeans rushed up to me saying, "Step back inside!" I obeyed his command, and asked him what the problem was. He asked me to step back out the door again and the alarm did not come on. He looked embarrassed and stated, "It must not have alarmed for you." So the bottom line was that whoever in the crowd had shoplifted walked away clean because the store security person could only focus on me as a suspect.

Even though segregation and racism continue to exist, blacks should turn this race problem over to God as America's race problem, and not theirs alone. At this late date it is so hard to discuss the past evils and even the present ones without someone's feelings being hurt. Therefore, I feel it would be in the best interest for blacks to continue trying to tell our past. As the old folks used to say, "In order for us to change the way things are, we first must understand how they came to be."

Now after twenty-seven years as cofounder with Dr. Hannibal Williams of Liberation House Alcohol and Drug Recovery Home, I can still feel the pain of humiliation and degradation from all races of people. Beginning with the humanly impossible, but with the power of God, I could accomplish the requirements for Liberation House's first contract with the city and county of San

Francisco for alcohol treatment. I believe that I have been turned away by many funding agencies because they thought that Liberation House was for black male alcoholics only. But I always had an open mind that men of all races, colors, creeds, and nationalities were welcome if they had a sincere desire to obtain sobriety and remain sober. Not two societies, one black, one white—separate and unequal. Therefore, in spite of receiving rejection from both blacks and whites, I stand fast that the Fourteenth Amendment, which was written for the Negroes in 1863, was a moral victory for people of all races and colors. From childhood until the present, I have believed that segregation and racism can never be equal. Thurgood Marshall of the NAACP, who was later appointed to the United States Supreme Court, fought so hard in 1953 when he took the Harry Briggs case of North Carolina and four more states before the Supreme Court. And he won over the renowned attorney John W. Davis, who was defending the old law of segregation—separate but unequal.

I have worked every position at Liberation House with the counsel and prayers of my wife, Florence, and Dr. Williams. I felt that I was doing an adequate job; however, many times I had to fight against dissident board members who did not want me to be a chairman of the board. In the past twenty-five years, to one degree or another, I have assisted in helping over 10,000 residents who have passed through Liberation House. There have been nine directors, and I have served as the tenth since 1992.

Alcoholism has been and continues to be the subject of intense research in an ongoing effort to try to determine the factors contributing to its onset. I wish that society would expend more effort on prevention by way of education, rather than incarceration. The truth is simply that the body has lost its ability to control alcohol, which becomes a self-diagnosing disease by the admission of the individual that he or she has become addicted. It is at this juncture that sobriety and recovery can follow, when the individual has discovered the truth about him or herself. Only the truth through God can set you free.

At this point, the alcoholic should fully understand the three concepts of addiction—physical, psychological, and spiritual—which, if thoroughly followed, can also be understood by attending AA meetings. I must confess that I am powerless over alcohol, and alcohol is powerless over my Higher Power, whom I know as God. In order to remain sober, we never drink alcohol again or use addicting drugs, because our addiction is only asleep until we wake it by drinking or using drugs again. I am convinced that God has kept me sober these past twenty-seven years. He will also do it for you.

About the Author

Mr. Curtis Jones is a positive role model and a positive influence in my life, and in his organization. The standards Mr. Jones has set for others have me overwhelmed with ambitions and aspirations to become the best that I can become. It is with his and his staff's support that I am currently attending two community colleges in pursuit of my counseling degrees.

Mr. Jones' compassion, empathy, and spirituality are uplifting, and I am honored to know this gentleman and be an alumnus of the program he co-founded, Liberation House. Mr. Jones has helped create history, not only for the African-American culture but also for the recovery culture as a whole. Faced with adversities, trials and tribulations, Mr. Jones faced his challenges head-on, once he learned the tools he needed to succeed in life, and now he has a legacy to be left on this earth for years to come.

Read about his life and the road he once took, and the road he chose to take over twenty-five years ago. Mr. Jones is an inspiration to many in the recovery world. I am grateful to have a historical figure as one of my friends and a guiding light. Thank you, Mr. Jones, for Liberation House and this treasured book.

Sincerely,

Frank-

A Grateful Recovering Addict